D0866824

Cambridge Texts and Studies in the History of Education

GENERAL EDITORS

A. C. F. BEALES, A. V. JUDGES, J. P. C. ROACH

JAMES MILL ON EDUCATION

IN THIS SERIES

TEXTS

Fénelon on Education edited by H. C. Barnard

Friedrich Froebel translated and edited by Irene Lilley

Matthew Arnold and the Education of the New Order edited by Peter Smith and Geoffrey Summerfield

Robert Owen on Education edited by Harold Silver

James Mill on Education edited by W. H. Burston

STUDIES

Education and the French Revolution by H. C. Barnard

OTHER VOLUMES IN PREPARATION

JAMES MILL
ON
EDUCATION

Edited by

W. H. BURSTON
Reader in Education
University of London Institute of Education

CAMBRIDGE
AT THE UNIVERSITY PRESS
1969

Published by the Syndics of the Cambridge University Press
Bentley House, 200 Euston Road, London N.W.1.
American Branch: 32 East 57th Street, New York, N.Y. 10022

Library of Congress Catalogue Card Number: 69–11268

Standard Book Number: 521 07414 2

Printed in Great Britain
by Unwin Brothers Limited
Woking and London

CONTENTS

EDITOR'S PREFACE

I am indebted to the family of the late Professor F. A. Cavenagh, who in 1931 edited *James and J. S. Mill on Education*, for permission to quote extensively from his Preface, and to use some of his Notes.

In the present volume the text of the essay *Education* is taken from the collection of *Essays on Government, Jurisprudence etc.* published in 1828. That for *Schools for All*, which appears for the first time in a modern edition, is taken from the original article published in the *Philanthropist*, 1812.

W. H. B.

INTRODUCTION

James Mill's life falls into four fairly easily defined stages. He was born in Scotland in 1773 and stayed there until 1802. From 1802 to 1808 is his first period in London: he was conventional, rather right-wing, and earned his living as a journalist. The third stage, 1808–1819, is marked by a close friendship with Jeremy Bentham. From 1819 to 1836 Mill had financial independence and security from his post as a civil servant in the East India Company.

His first twenty-nine years in Scotland are important. His father was a shoemaker: his mother was socially ambitious for her son, who was able and rapidly attracted first the friendship and later the patronage of wealthier people. As a result of the kindness of the greatest of these benefactors, Sir John Stuart, James Mill spent seven years at the University of Edinburgh and emerged licensed as a preacher. His course of study covered most of the subjects of the day, including natural science, but its emphasis was on philosophy, especially Greek philosophy, for which the classical language courses were a preliminary. The later training in theology also included philosophy. In this period of Mill's life the important points to notice are that he had a highly conventional and rather strict upbringing of the kind which in a later age was characterised as Victorian respectability. Second, there is the stress in his university education on Greek philosophy. There is abundant evidence in Mill's Commonplace Book of the debt which he felt he owed to the Greek philosophers. And his education of his son placed a knowledge of the classical languages and of Greek philosophy as the basis of a sound education. Third, it should be noted that Mill's first, albeit brief, career was as a preacher. He was not at this time the agnostic he was later to become.

During his first six years in London there is no evidence of radical opinion or of unconventional beliefs. He joined a corps of defence volunteers to defend the country against Napoleon's projected invasion. He contributed to the *Literary Journal* and edited the *St. James Chronicle*. He married Harriet Burrow in 1805, and in 1806 the first of nine children was born and christened John Stuart Mill after his father's Scottish benefactor. Mill then gave up a good income from journalism in order to embark on a life of scholarship, and write the *History of British India*. This task, which he thought would take three years, in fact took eleven, and made these eleven years of his life a period of financial penury.

The year 1808 is therefore important for this reason, and even more important for the development of Mill's thought, for it is in this year that he met Jeremy Bentham. Their friendship rapidly became close and Mill and his growing family spent several months of each summer with Bentham in the country—during the four years 1814–18 at Ford Abbey in Somerset. Mill also became a tenant and next-door neighbour of Bentham's in Queen's Square Place (now Queen Anne's Gate), Westminster. Early in their friendship Mill became an uncompromising advocate of political utilitarianism, demanding that all governments should be judged by the test of 'utility'—whether they promoted the greatest happiness of the greatest number of people, and a succession of articles in the *Edinburgh Review* between 1808 and 1813 bore witness to his conversion. All this time, however, he was working on his *History of British India*: this was completed in 1817, published, and by the reputation he thus gained, and by the assiduous efforts of his friends, he was appointed an examiner in the East India Office, in 1819, at a salary of £800 a year. His financial anxieties were over.

From 1819 to the end of his life in 1836, Mill rose progressively in the East India Office, becoming its head in 1830. The work was not very onerous, and it is in this period that Mill wrote his major works—the *Analysis of the Human Mind* commenced in 1822 and published in 1828, and the *Fragment on Mackintosh*, a book of some 400 pages defending his moral philosophy, published in 1835. He also published articles throughout this period on such subjects as the state of the nation, the ballot, reform of the church, and the aristocracy—all these indicate his continuing interest in the current political scene. The two major works are philosophical but his interest in the philosophy of utilitarianism really started earlier, in 1815, when he was engaged in writing the article *Education* for the *Encyclopedia Britannica*. This and other articles for the *Encyclopedia* were subsequently published as a collection of essays on different aspects of utilitarian thought, and became the basis of much earnest discussion among radically minded people. The article on education is the first of the two essays reprinted in this volume.

During his life Mill showed a practical interest in education at three major points. First, he was an early advocate of the monitorial system of teaching by which a master taught the older boys and they in turn taught the rest in small and homogeneous groups of ten or so.

Second, following his wide definition of 'education' as meaning total environmental influence, he took sole charge of the education of his eldest son John Stuart Mill and controlled his whole environment and curriculum of study. James Mill's belief in the educational value of the monitorial system is illustrated by the fact that he used it progressively for the education of his own children. Third, he was concerned in the founding of University College, London, and as a member of its council was active in its affairs during its early years. Of all these activities the one which involved most public controversy was the first. Mill advocated non-sectarian schools: the Church of England retaliated by demanding church control of education. Mill set forth his views in characteristically pungent language in an article in the *Philanthropist* in 1812. This article was subsequently published as a pamphlet entitled *Schools for All, in preference to Schools for Churchmen only*, and this is the second work reprinted in this volume.

'An article in an Encyclopedia' wrote Mill to his friend Ricardo, 'should be to a certain degree didactic, and also elementary—as being to be consulted by the ignorant as well as the knowing; but the matter that has been often explained, may be passed over very shortly, to leave more space for that which is less commonly known. As for space, you should take much or little, just as the matter requires.'[1] As we read through the essay *Education*, our first reflection might be that very long passages are devoted to factors affecting physical health, and that these would hardly be thought to require that degree of emphasis and length of treatment

[1] *Works and Correspondence of David Ricardo*, ed. P. Sraffa (Cambridge, 1955), no. 325, Mill to Ricardo, 11 September 1819.

today. Their significance is not so much what they say, as that it was thought necessary to say it as 'that which is less commonly known'. They are a commentary on the poverty and neglect of the age.

The modern reader will concentrate on the philosophical aspects of the essay, and he will find here a model of what a theory of education should be, whether or not he agrees with Mill's particular conclusions. For any theory should make explicit two main problems. First it should state an aim or purpose and perhaps say why that aim should be preferable to alternatives. Second it has to concern itself with the nature of the pupil and his abilities, and with the learning process. The first of these is a problem of moral philosophy, since it is concerned with what *ought* to be, or what is desirable. The second is a problem of psychology—of examining the nature of the pupil or, as Mill put it, the 'phenomena of the human mind'. Mill's essay deals with both these matters clearly and incisively, but he adds a new field of enquiry with his very wide definition of education as 'everything which affects those qualities of mind on which happiness depends, from the first germ of existence to the final extinction of life'. He thus regarded education as much more than formal schooling, and on this basis developed his concepts of social and political education, or the educative influence of society and the state respectively on the individual members of the community.

Mill's statement of the aims of education is in the very first sentence of the essay: it is to 'render the individual, as much as possible, an instrument of happiness, first to himself, and next to other beings'. Later, in section II, he lists the qualities of mind on which happiness depends as intelligence, temperance, justice and generosity. Here we have the familiar utilitarian aim and criterion of conduct—that actions are right in so far as they promote the greatest happiness of the greatest number of people. This is the moral ideal and it therefore follows that education should equip people to attain it.

If we look carefully at the sentence in which Mill defines the aim of education, we shall find not one but two aims: the individual must first be educated to find his own happiness, as well as to bring happiness to others. This statement we may find in itself unexceptionable, until we reflect on its major implication which is that neither pursuit comes naturally and education is needed for both. And this is particularly important when we put the first aim—education for personal happiness—alongside James Mill's strong belief in psychological hedonism—that man always and inevitably seeks his own pleasure. 'Pleasure,' he wrote, 'is the end, and *generally speaking*, the only end'[1] of all human behaviour. If this is so, why does man need education to achieve it? An obvious answer to this, that Mill meant by 'happiness' something different from 'pleasure' can hardly be supported by the evidence. Although in section III of the essay Mill argues that we do not yet know 'wherein human happiness consists', and although he repeats this assertion in the *Fragment on Mackintosh*[2], he often uses the two terms synonymously, and the weight of the evidence, in all his public and private writing, is certainly that he regarded them as interchangeable. Certainly if 'happiness' had a special meaning, distinct from 'pleasure', it would be essential to the utilitarian doctrine to define and expound it.

[1] *Fragment on Mackintosh* (1870 edn.), p. 360.
[2] *Ibid.* Appendix A, p. 394.

This being so, it is important to look closely, when examining Mill's doctrine of education for personal happiness, at what he has to say about 'pleasure'. Pleasure is defined as the 'object of desire' and desire is defined as 'the idea of a pleasure'.[1] It is therefore not possible to sustain the obvious objection that we sometimes desire things for other reasons than pleasure, for on Mill's definition this is impossible—'pleasure' is a generic term. In our language 'satisfaction' of desire would perhaps be a better equivalent. If this is accepted, we can explain a central point in Mill's argument, namely that we should not merely seek personal pleasure, but that it is our duty to maximise it. As it stands this seems absurd, for I can hardly be held to be failing in my duty if I do not attain the greatest personal pleasure. But Mill's comments in *Education* (p. 63, below) are quite clear: 'If [a man] has any appetite in his nature which leads him to pursue certain things with which the most effectual pursuit of happiness is inconsistent . . . evil is incurred. A perfect command, then, over a man's appetites and desires . . . which . . . enables him to pursue constantly what he deliberately approves, is indispensably requisite to enable him to produce the greatest possible quantity of happiness.' And there is other evidence to the same effect. To Francis Place, concerned about the education of his daughter, he wrote: 'Above all think of her happiness solely, without one jot of passion being allowed to step into the scale.'[2] This is a curious adjuration to a fond parent: it can only be explained, as can the passage in *Education*, on the basis that not merely pleasure, of any kind, should be pursued, or

[1] *Analysis of the Human Mind* (2nd edn., 1878), II, 192.
[2] B. M. Addn. MSS. 35,152, Mill to Place, 22 September 1816.

that every 'desire and appetite' should be gratified, but that maximum pleasure should be sought. And his son, writing of his father, confirms this: 'Temperance, in the large sense intended by the Greek philosophers, was with him . . . almost the central point of educational precept.'[1] This again is a counsel against seeking every pleasure—most pleasures, his son wrote, he thought were 'overvalued': what was needed was to maximise pleasure. It is clear that we have to take this point seriously.

It is much more arguable, and much more reasonable if we look at the problem from the point of view of desires and satisfactions. What Mill is then advocating is that we should cultivate the highest kind of desires because we should find in the end that these yield the greatest satisfaction or pleasure. To do this we need the quality of temperance or self-control over our appetites and various fleeting desires, so that we pursue only what we 'deliberately approve'. So far the argument is at least plausible but it raises another difficulty. As Mill himself pointed out, in an unpublished dialogue in his Commonplace Book,[2] if we talk of higher forms of pleasure, of different qualities of desire, we are 'taking a different ground for our approbation' than merely pleasure, simple and unqualified. Does not this invalidate the utilitarian ideal that pleasure or happiness, simple and unqualified, is the only test of goodness?

What Mill concluded was that the cultivation of the highest desires would yield the greatest satisfaction—in his language, the greatest *quantity* of pleasure: therefore there was no need for any other criterion of the good

[1] J. S. Mill, *Autobiography* (World's Classics, 1924), p. 40.
[2] Dialogue on Drama, in Commonplace Book, vol. IV.

than pleasure, providing it was maximised. His first aim in education thus was not merely personal pleasure, but *maximum* personal pleasure, an aim to be achieved by cultivating the power of self-denial, so that pursuit of passing pleasures should not deflect us from the more satisfying long-term pleasures. It is a self-realisation theory of ethics: we cultivate the highest parts of our nature, because, in the end, they are the most satisfying. A remark in the *Essay on Government* shews the true line of Mill's thought, when he speaks of 'the middling rank' exemplifying 'all that has most exalted and refined human nature'.[1]

We may now turn to the second more familiar part of the utilitarian ideal—the promotion of the general happiness—in the light of this discussion. Since Mill identifies his aim in education with his general moral ideal for conduct, there are one or two points which need to be noticed about it as a statement of an ideal. The first is, does he mean by 'pleasure' the same thing when he speaks of our giving it to others, as he meant when speaking of our personal pleasure. Should we give to others the higher forms of pleasure (which he would call the greatest quantity of pleasure) or should we give them what they want, which might not be what was best for them? On the other hand, there is little doubt that Mill was an individualist, and as such would hold that each person must be the final judge of where his or her own happiness lay. He seems to have resolved the conflict in his own mind by his faith that the example of the 'middling ranks' would be followed—a faith which might strike us as far-fetched, but it was not unjustified in the England of his time. G. M. Young has written: 'The Evangelicals gave the island

[1] *Essay on Government*, ed. E. Barker (Cambridge, 1937), p. 72.

a creed which was at once the basis of its morality and the justification of its wealth and power . . . By about 1830 their work was done . . . They had established a certain level of behaviour for all who wished to stand well with their fellows. In moralizing society, they had made social disapproval a force which the boldest sinner might fear.'[1] James Mill was not an Evangelical, but his early upbringing and his ascetic tastes had made him fit well into the cult of Victorian respectability. And his faith in the educative power of the 'middling ranks' was more a shrewd observation of what happened in his own day, than a faith.

A second question to ask about the utilitarian ideal concerns the principle of equality which it apparently includes. The test of good conduct is not merely that it should promote the general happiness, but that such happiness should be equally distributed, 'everyone to count for one and none for more than one'. It is difficult to maintain that this is not an additional principle: one can imagine situations in which the total general happiness was not increased if equal distribution of pleasure is insisted upon. Yet if it is conceded that equality is an extraneous principle, the utilitarians cannot claim, as they do, that the greatest happiness is the sole test of goodness.

Finally there is the question whether the motives from which we act are important or relevant in assessing the moral quality of our actions. Since utilitarianism maintains that actions are right if they produce the greatest happiness, it appears to follow that it is the *results* or consequences of actions which are important: so long as these consequences are beneficial the motive which prompts the action is irrelevant. Mill does not

[1] *Early Victorian England*, ed. G. M. Young, II, p. 416.

deal directly with this point in *Education*, but he makes some apparently inconsistent remarks in the *Fragment on Mackintosh*. Here he insists that 'morality is an attribute of intention' and then continues: 'acts are virtuous if good to others is intended, though it be not the motive to the act. They are virtuous in a still higher degree if good to others is also the motive.'[1]

Here we reach not a minor but a major inconsistency, for it is essentially the inconsistency between utilitarianism—the duty of promoting the general happiness—and psychological hedonism—the doctrine that man is inevitably a selfish pursuer of his own pleasure. Mill has three answers to this, none of which is really satisfactory. He argues, first, that a child should be taught from the earliest days to associate its own greatest pleasure with that of those around him; second, that we all have a great desire for the favourable regard of others, presumably only to be obtained by giving them pleasure;[2] and third, that in analysing what we would now call 'other-regarding' sentiments into their original selfish origins, he is not altering their genuinely unselfish nature once they are formed—'gratitude remains gratitude, generosity, generosity, after analysis the same as before',[3] he retorted. None of these arguments resolves the difficulty. If a child associates his own pleasure with that of others, his motives are none the less selfish. If we gain pleasure from the favourable regard of others, our motive remains selfish. And sentiments such as generosity cannot be hedonistic in origin, and unselfish when developed. Either the hedonistic origins persist, and

[1] *Fragment on Mackintosh*, p. 394.

[2] *Education*, pp. 98–9, 115–16, below.

[3] *Fragment on Mackintosh*, p. 51.

psychological hedonism as a doctrine is upheld, or they do not, and man is not by nature selfish. If Mill insists on his psychological hedonism, and there is plenty of evidence that he does, then his account of the motives to right action is not in terms of a moral motive but in terms of hitching selfish desires to a moral star.

Thus Mill's moral philosophy is fundamentally inconsistent with a major element in his psychology. Yet there is, I believe, an explanation, though not a justification, of this inconsistency, if we consider the England of his day. It was in his view a highly corrupt society in which men were intent on pursuing their own interests, safeguarding their privileges and advancing their personal fortunes. In such a society men's motives were irretrievably selfish, and any practical programme for reform would have to be based on this assumption. And utilitarianism in general had always a dual purpose: to be at once a statement of the ideal and a practical criterion for immediate reform. Therefore, in the contemporary situation, one must use the existing selfish motives to promote good, by devices such as representative government, for if the selfish interests of all were represented, none could be disregarded, and government for the general good would result. And this is also the basis of Mill's individualism, for if all were selfish none could be trusted to say where another's pleasure lay. But in an ideal society things would be different: appropriate education would have taught everyone to seek the general pleasure, because they themselves desired it.

The other inconsistencies are also more understandable if we remember the widespread poverty of Mill's day, as witness his own comments on the bad harvest of 1816: 'There must now be of necessity a very deficient crop and very high prices—and these with unexampled scarcity of work will produce a degree of misery, the thought of which makes the flesh creep on one's bones—one-third of the people must die.'[1] In these circumstances there was little conflict between what people wanted and what, ideally, they ought to have: such a dichotomy belongs essentially to an affluent society. And in the same poverty-stricken society there can be little doubt that the most effective immediate contribution to the general happiness would be a more equitable distribution of material benefits. It is perhaps because of this that Mill took the principle of equality for granted. Finally, we can see why he speaks in two voices about motives and consequences of actions and their importance to morality. Granted that motives in existing society were bad, the only practicable test of goodness must lie in the consequences of actions. But good education could produce good motives and conduct would become 'still more virtuous'. It is clear therefore that these difficulties with Mill's moral ideal are both relevant and important when that ideal is considered as an aim of education. It is by education that the child will learn where true happiness lies and it is by education that he will learn not only to seek it for himself but to desire it for others. And there is a further implication for education. It is central to Mill's moral theory that people should be able to anticipate correctly the consequences of their actions and he therefore demands that intelligence should be one of the qualities which education should cultivate. And we get a clear indication of Mill's belief in the principle of equality when he demands that,

[1] *Correspondence of David Ricardo*, no. 175, Mill to Ricardo, 14 August 1816.

despite the necessity for the majority of the people to do manual labour, all should be educated until the age of fifteen or sixteen, so that all might perceive where true happiness lay, and all might act with intelligence to promote the general happiness.

James Mill's psychological theory is set out in section I of *Education* and developed in detail in his later work—the *Analysis of the Human Mind*. The theory follows the English empirical tradition of John Locke and others, that all knowledge is derived from sense-experience and from our introspective experience of our own feelings. Mill uses the term 'feelings' as a generic word to cover both sets of experience—of our own emotions, and, through the five senses, of the external world. He also uses the word 'idea' to mean what we would now call an 'image', i.e., the re-collection of a sense impression.

To this foundation of knowledge, Mill adds the principle of the association of ideas. It is a common experience to find that one thing may recall another—in wondering where we left an umbrella we may recall images of quite different things simply because we experienced them with the umbrella or in association with one another. Such an association of ideas, in our modern use of the term, is quite capricious. Mill extends the concept very widely and uses it, first as a weapon of analysis, and second as an explanation of categories of thought such as causation. Thus he argues that our idea of a rose which appears to be a simple sensation is in fact a complex one containing what sight, smell and touch tell us about a rose. Since all three are normally experienced together they become associated. And the idea of a 'cause' is also held to be an example of association. If we say that heat will cause metal to expand it is simply because whenever we have seen heat applied to metal it has expanded. If we take the logician's definition of cause—whenever A is present B must follow—we can see that there is a plausible case for Mill's contention that causation is an example of invariable association, in our experience, of A with B.

Mill's use of the association principle as a weapon of analysis arises from his desire to construct a mental science analogous to physical science; hence he sought to reduce the phenomena of the human mind to their smallest atomic elements. And he felt that, in the association principle, he had found something like the fundamental laws of physical science—a single all-pervading principle of explanation.[1] For this reason Mill's 'association psychology' is not entirely correctly named, for it was not intended purely as a psychology, certainly not as we should understand it now; though, since it purports to give an account of the *origins* of our ideas and concepts, it does imply some ideas about the learning process, and it is therefore fair to examine it from the psychological point of view.

If this is to be done, we must look at another and even more strongly held conviction of James Mill—his belief in psychological hedonism—the theory that everyone was by nature selfish. This was connected with association psychology in his mind, and he writes in *Education:* 'Two things . . . have a wonderful power over the sequences [associations]. They are Custom and Pain and Pleasure' (p. 58, below). If we associate two things sufficiently often, as for example by daily

[1] Cf. J. S. Mill's Preface to the *Analysis of the Human Mind* (2nd edn., 1878), vol. I, especially pp. v–xii.

habit, the association will be a firm one. But it will also be firm if there is a pleasurable result. But pleasure is the end or object and the intermediate stages or means may be good or bad. It is the business of education to ensure that these means are beneficent and good rather than harmful. Thus all men may desire wealth which brings pleasure, but it may be gained by fair or foul means—education should ensure that it is always associated with 'the acquisition of rare and useful qualities . . . and steady industry'.

As a theory of learning, associationism is traditionally criticised on three grounds. First, it is argued that it is purely mechanical: the mind absorbs without discrimination the environment which it experiences. But as a matter of introspective fact we do not perceive all that is present to the senses: we select and attend to some things and ignore others. Second, most people would say that the process of perception was not purely mechanical: motivation affects what we notice—for instance, we notice what interests us. Finally, associationism as set forth by Mill is an extreme form of environmentalism—men's abilities and characters owe little or nothing to inherited factors, all is the product of the environment. It is to be noted that Mill quotes with approval Helvétius' famous comment: 'l'éducation peut tout': if he did not claim quite so much himself, he would none the less have substantially agreed.

With the first of these criticisms, we have to ask just what is meant by the term 'mechanical'. Its main implication is that the phenomena of human knowledge and behaviour are to be explained in terms of 'causes' as used in the scientific sense. The general form of such an explanation we have already noted, that whenever

A is present B must follow, and whenever B is present A must have preceded. As such, any such scientific explanation is sharply different from explaining human behaviour in terms of purpose, intention or desire, and of course, of any free choice.

Since Mill's avowed purpose is to create a science of the human mind, he often writes in the language and terminology of science, especially in his larger work on psychology. But this language obscures the true meaning of his theory of association, for the introduction of the pain–pleasure principle makes a fundamental change in the theory. Pleasure is an end or goal, and an explanation of behaviour governed by pursuit of pleasure is in these terms. It is an explanation in which the 'cause' of human behaviour lies in an intention or motive, which people are free to have and to pursue as they like. It is sharply different from scientific or mechanistic explanation, for instance in looking not at preceding factors but rather at results or consequences as the explanation of actions.

Not only is pleasure as a motive central to Mill's psychology: his moral philosophy requires a psychological theory in terms of purpose and not in terms of mechanism. For he requires people to pursue the general happiness, including their own, and demands that all actions should be judged by how far they promote this purpose. Strictly speaking, such a theory of morals has no room for moral principles or rules, for all such rules are provisional only: the test of every particular action is whether it promotes the general happiness. It may be generally true that it is wrong to tell lies, and that the general happiness is promoted, normally, by following this rule or principle: on occasion, as in deceiving a seriously ill patient, it may be right to break the rule. The utilitarian would regard such action as justified since to him all actions should be the result of calculation as to whether or not they promoted the general happiness. Yet the formation of good habits, the adoption of invariable rules and principles of conduct would be the kind of moral training most readily taught by means of association psychology, as Mill himself indicates in *Education* when he speaks of the value to religious habits of mind of the custom of grace before meals. Whenever a particular action recalled a rule, we would automatically follow the rule. I would maintain therefore that Mill's moral theory, which was the reverse of this, required something very different from a mechanistic theory of the mind as its psychological basis. It was his desire to found a science which led him to speak so often in mechanistic terms and to talk, for instance, of 'rendering the human mind an *instrument* of happiness'. But the true meaning of his psychology is different: it is a teleological theory (i.e. oriented towards purpose) and its most central precept is not associationism as it is normally understood, but hedonism.

If this is accepted, then the other criticisms of associationism need to be reconsidered. If pleasure can determine the strength of an association, then logically it might also determine what we select to perceive, what interests us and so on. Thus Mill could admit selective perception without being false to the particular meaning he gave to associationism. And, of course, motivation would, from early childhood, determine what associations were formed. Finally, our rejection of the theory that Mill was a mechanical associationist has some relevance to how far and in what way he should be regarded as a believer in the power of environment. On a strictly mechanical view of association, the environment would go on affecting people throughout life; and later associations, if they were experienced sufficiently frequently, would rapidly outweigh and eradicate earlier ones. It may be that Mill, with his wide definition of 'education' and his theory that society was an agent of education, inclined to this view. But if pleasure is brought in as affecting the strength of an association, it is possible to argue that the educator of someone in his formative years is in a commanding position, and able to give or withhold that pleasure at will. There is then an alternative view possible, though still environmentalist—namely that environment is supremely important in the early and formative years of life and can then form associations, traits of character and so forth, which will last and withstand later social pressures. In the essay Mill seems to subscribe to this view, though it seems more a product of observation and common sense on his part, than a realisation of the logical consequence of marrying association psychology with hedonism. We thus have evidence that he supported both forms of environmentalism: which of the two accords more with his theory in general depends upon an examination of his concepts of social and political education.

Mill's doctrine of social and political education (set out in section IV of the essay) is a theory of the educative effects of society and the state upon the individuals in the community. In this context the word 'education' is used in a neutral and descriptive sense, and not as commendatory, for it is clear that Mill thought society could have bad effects—he is indeed more successful in portraying these than in expounding the good effects of an ideal society. The theory is important for its obvious implication that formal schooling, and early family upbringing, can have only a limited and perhaps temporary effect. It is also important in elucidating Mill's psychological theory: if we ascribe importance to a mechanical form of association, then the doctrines of social and political education logically follow, for later associations, if repeated sufficiently frequently, will eradicate earlier ones.

Mill gives two means by which society exercises its influence: first, the principle of imitation and, second, the power of society over the happiness and misery of its members. The first is self-explanatory and could be based on association psychology. The second rests on a hedonistic basis, for it argues that people will cultivate those qualities which are rewarded, or, to use the phrase which constantly recurs in Mill's correspondence, that 'men pursue their own interests'. It also postulates someone in a position to reward the qualities which it is desired to encourage, and, in a bad society, that those qualities will be rewarded which safeguard the power and privilege of the ruling group. Both these assumptions require examination.

A man may be said to act in his own interest if he seeks something such as personal wealth, which brings benefit to him alone. But he may also be said to be 'pursuing his interest' if he amasses wealth for the sake of his family or for any other cause in which he is interested. He may desire to educate his children privately: in one sense, he is pursuing his own interest if he furthers this aim. The difference between the two senses of 'pursuing one's interest' is that, in seeking wealth for ourselves, we are pursuing an *object* which is selfish in itself, and in seeking wealth for some other cause in which we are interested we are speaking not of the *object* we pursue, but of the *motive* from which we pursue any object. The phrase 'pursuing one's interest' is thus dangerously ambiguous and the argument that men invariably do so may, in the hands of a psychological hedonist, easily become tautologous. If a man acts invariably to produce his own pleasure, it follows that, whatever he does, his own pleasure is the motive: we assume what we have to prove, we infer the motive not from the object sought but from an *a priori* article of faith, that man always seeks his own pleasure.

When Mill speaks of 'the rewards which society has to bestow' it is clear enough that he means material rewards appealing to man's selfish nature. But his meaning is less clear when he speaks of 'the intense desire we feel for the favourable regards of mankind'—in short, for other people's approbation. As a general proposition, one might remark that other people's approbation would hardly be accorded to selfish people and it would follow that *unselfish* behaviour would be the means of pursuing this particular form of 'one's own interest'—in short, it would illustrate the ambiguity we have just discussed. But it may none the less be a genuine and influential motive in mankind in general. Certainly in Mill's day, social disapproval was a powerful force, and in his *Essay on Jurisprudence* he argued that publicity for criminal conviction would be a most potent punishment.[1]

For these reasons people have an irresistible tendency to conform to the society in which they live, and society can properly be called an educator. But this raises the

[1] *Essay on Jurisprudence*, pp. 21 ff.

second question: what precisely is meant by the term 'society'? We can think of 'society' as the personal group with whom we live and work and pass our leisure time: when Mill talks of imitation he is clearly thinking along these lines. But his theory in general requires him to apply it to society as a whole and to talk of the social influence of a national community. Can we talk of this without postulating some agreement obtaining throughout that society as to what qualities would obtain 'its favourable regard'?

In Mill's day, one could make this assumption because of the all-powerful position of the landowners and their pervading influence at local and national levels, both directly and through the associated institution of the established church. Mill argued that such influence was corrupting and designed to ensure the continuance of the privileges of the ruling group. Whether and how the theory of social education applies to other kinds of society is not so clear. In a pure democracy, would there be a ruling group? In a free society, would there be that degree of conformity to accepted values that G. M. Young noted in Mill's day? On the other hand we do detect general qualities in such societies, and virtues such as tolerance may be widely diffused and generally praised, even though their result is the reverse of promoting an orthodoxy. Mill's theory deserves to be considered as a general theory if only because we all make assumptions about the power of different forms of education to change society, and this he would deny. But it must be said that, as it stands, it is more a comment on his day than a well-thought-out theory of general application.

'Political Education', says Mill, 'is like the keystone

of the arch.' What he means is that the state or 'political machine' determines the form which society takes, has supreme power, and controls all the big rewards which the community has to offer. This idea would be challenged by most political theorists nowadays, and some certainly would argue that the economic organisation of society tended to determine its political shape. To them, Mill's view appears naïve. But it was not only typical of his age, it was true of his society. The most powerful economic forces—the landowners—were not a secret vested interest operating behind the political machine, they *were* the political machine, and were openly in control of all the sources of political power. Thus Mill, like the Chartists later, thought political reform the essential preliminary to any other kind of reform.

When he speaks of political education it is mainly in terms of the political machine having control of material rewards, of being able to satisfy 'the grand objects of desire' and therefore of being able to foster those qualities of which it approved. Like social education, it depends on man's hedonistic nature and on the existence of a ruling group in a position to offer rewards. This illustrates Mill's eighteenth-century outlook. In an article, he set out what an ideal aristocracy might be, but he never contemplated a society in which there was no aristocracy; and it is fair to comment that it is not clear, as he expounds it, how his theory of social and political education would work in a pure democracy. What is clear is that he felt the theory to be important and of general application. In his Commonplace Book he recorded: 'Society and the Government the grand instruments of education—a fine passage to prove this in Plato's VIth book of the

Republic.' To Mill, this was a fundamental truth of political and social theory and an essential part of educational theory.

An important feature of both social and political education, as Mill saw it, was not the direct but the indirect influence which these two forces had over the characters of both parents and teachers, in charge respectively of domestic and technical education. In general the point follows logically from his theory: if education is defined as the influence of environment, and people in general are subject to it, then parents and teachers are as much influenced by society and the state as anyone else. But although Mill does not mention it when speaking of social education, it seems to me that he is making not only the general point but an important particular one as well. In the preceding section on schooling, he concludes with some remarks on 'several causes which tend to impair the utility of old and opulent establishments of education'. They love ease and tend to give value to trifles and so on. But all these evils 'are apt to be indefinitely increased when they are united with an ecclesiastical establishment, because, whatever the vices of the ecclesiastical system, the universities have in that case an interest to bend the whole of their force to the support of those vices, and to that end to vitiate the human mind, which can only be rendered the friend of abuses in proportion as it is vitiated intellectually, or morally, or both' (p. 113, below). What he says of universities would also be true of schools and he is here speaking of an institution in society, namely the established church, directly moulding to its ways the education which its satellite establishments conduct.

In this sense the pamphlet *Schools for all* may be seen as a particular illustration of this aspect of his theory of social and political education. This is, of course, not its only importance, and to understand it, we must look briefly at the context in which it was written.

In England, in the first quarter of the nineteenth century the provision of education was sporadic and capricious—it was as likely not to exist at all as to be there. In this, England stood in marked contrast to Scotland, where primary schools existed in every parish; and this contrast was not lost on James Mill. Perhaps because of this, and perhaps because the problem of education became acute with the rapid rise of child population at the time, Mill became an ardent champion of educational reform and ceaselessly urged the provision of primary education for all. This campaign preceded by several years the writing of *Education*, but, as we have noted, his educational theory in the essay obliged him to postulate some education for all.

In view of the magnitude of the gap between the child population and the provision of schools, primary education for all would have been an impossible task in the immediate future but for one factor. This was the discovery and popularisation of the monitorial system. Before we condemn this as a makeshift measure, we should see it in its context. In the Edinburgh High School where the system was adopted, the Latin class numbered one hundred, and teaching took the form of hearing each boy construe individually.[1] To us, this would appear highly inefficient and a system of

[1] B.M. Addn. MSS. 27,823, Gray to Wakefield, 28 December 1813.

grading the pupils by ability into groups of ten, all learning simultaneously, was a major advance in method. Similarly with the small all-age schools in parts of England—there were five such schools in the Bow Street–Long Acre district in London—the problem was how to teach such disparate pupils and the monitorial system provided a solution. At any rate, both Bentham and James Mill supported the system on educational grounds.

It was claimed that Dr Bell of Madras had originally invented the monitorial system in 1798: in England it was popularised by a Quaker named Joseph Lancaster. An organisation called first the Royal Lancasterian Society and later the British and Foreign School Society was set up to develop monitorial primary schools all over the country. It attempted to avoid religious controversy by insisting on the Bible as the sole source of religious instruction and by a strict avoidance of denominational teaching. But it did not succeed in this: there were vigorous protests from sections of the Church of England who, in 1811, set up their own National Society for establishing denominational primary schools. The dispute between the two organisations is recorded in the columns of the *Quarterly Review*, supporting the Church of England, and the *Philanthropist* and *Edinburgh Review*, supporting Lancaster.

James Mill and Francis Place were untiring supporters of the Lancasterian 'schools for all' and Mill wrote in their defence in the *Edinburgh Review* in 1813. His central argument is always a severely practical one: if denominational schools have to be established, then two or more will be required in every village in the country and every district in the towns, and this doubles or trebles the task of providing primary education for all. With so many children getting no education at all, Mill saw in the demand for sectarian schools something which would make an already enormous problem impossible of solution. To the modern reader, this argument seems unanswerable. But in the climate of opinion of the day it was radical, for much educational work had been done by religious bodies and all agreed that religion was something which children should be taught. Inside the Lancasterian movement for example, a bitter quarrel broke out between those who thought that children should be taught to read the Bible and those who thought that it should be the only book they read[1]—it is hard for the modern reader to understand such a dispute. And when figures are available, it is clear that Church of England children formed a large part, and in some cases a majority, of the pupils at Lancasterian schools,[2] and this perhaps explains, though it may not justify, the angry reaction of the zealots of the established church.

James Mill was not concerned with the argument over reading the Bible, for he firmly believed that teaching children to read was one thing and teaching them religion was quite another. One would expect that he himself, as an agnostic, would not even have wanted the Bible taught, as is illustrated by the education which he gave his own children.[3] But he saw the

[1] In practice, few Lancasterian schools restricted reading to the Bible.

[2] Cf. Place Collection, vol. 60. B.M. West London Lancasterian Association, 29 May 1815.

[3] Cf. J. S. Mill's *Autobiography*. But even here Mill was less dogmatic than is generally supposed: his daughters were regular church-goers (M. St. J. Packe, *Life of John Stuart Mill*, London, 1954, p. 25 and footnote).

need for compromise in practice in order to work with the Quakers who backed Lancaster, and he was in any case less extreme in his religious views than Bentham. Certainly, unlike Bentham, he published no condemnation of religion as such: on the contrary, in his later years an article of his, albeit a somewhat eccentric one, set forth how an efficient national church should be organised.[1]

Mill's objection was to the church as an organisation, and particularly to an established church. Thus, what may seem to us to be debating points in *Schools for All* represent some of Mill's most cherished convictions. When he argues that the church preferred ignorance to knowledge among the young, he is voicing a genuine belief. And when he demands that the test of utility be applied to the established church he is quite consistently applying the utilitarian criterion to a powerful social institution. Fortunately for him, he is able to quote Paley, a firm utilitarian of the Church of England, on his side, but Paley was by no means representative of general Anglican opinion.

To understand Mill's antipathy to the established church of his day, we should notice one or two features of its organisation. It was alone in Europe in demanding no professional qualification or knowledge of theology from its priests. And it was very closely linked with the landowners. According to Halévy, in 1815 eleven bishops were of noble birth and many had family connexions with the government. Of 11,700 benefices in England and Wales, only 1500 were in the gift of the bishop: of the rest, at least half were openly, and the remainder in practice, in the gift of the landowners. The situation was worsened by the failure of the

[1] 'The Church and its Reform', *London Review*, July 1835.

church to keep pace with the shift of population from the south to the north. The province of York contained 6 dioceses and 2,000 parishes: that of Canterbury, with a much smaller population, 20 dioceses and 10,000 parishes. Hence there were valuable livings in the south with little or no work attached to them: Cobbett discovered one in Wiltshire, worth £300 a year, with neither church nor vicarage. A consequence of this was pluralism: some priests held as many as eight livings, delegating such duties as there were to grossly underpaid curates.[1]

This, then, was the institution which found itself in danger from the Lancasterian movement and which sought to control the education of the young. To all these lamentable features was added one still worse in Mill's eyes—that it was the established church and thus linked openly with the state. As an abstract proposition, Mill thought this was bad for both partners. Government should be judged by the test of utility: if it was good it would be seen to be so and would not need the support of an extraneous and irrelevant institution. For the church, if it was linked with the state, must inevitably be inhibited in discharging its religious functions and it must tend to support the government whether good or bad. It could neither be an independent critic nor proclaim a moral ideal, for it was fatally compromised. In fact, concludes Mill, men only maintain establishments when it is to their interest to do so, and it is here that we shall find the true reason for the established church.

For in practice Mill had no doubt that the government of his day was corrupt:—

[1] Cf. E. Halévy, *History of the English People* (London, 1964 edn.), vol. I, part III, pp. 390–99.

Not a man is there, I fear in that house [he wrote to Ricardo about the House of Commons] who would not compromise the good of his country in many, and these far from trifling particulars, to gain the favour of a ministry, of a party, . . . or to push some other personal end . . . it is an easy thing to contract opinions which favour one's corrupt inclinations . . . It is curious to trace, even in those who seem to be the farthest removed from the hope of directly sharing in the plunder, by what secret links the opinions which favour misgovernment are really and in fact connected with the feelings of the plunderers: even by vain imitation . . . Even when education has produced all its effects, it requires some association or other with ideas of interest to make any man a convert to doctrines which would render the whole of the human race for ever slaves, for the benefit of a few. Yet these are doctrines which more than 99 in 100 of all the rich and great men in England perpetually preach: to such a degree by the operation of the bad principles of our government, are the intellectual and moral parts of the mind among the leading orders corrupted and depraved.[1]

Here was a view which Mill constantly reiterated: as he put it in a later letter, where men's duties and interests are 'not in concord, whence alone the performance of those duties can be expected', you will get bad government, directed towards personal privilege and advantage, and of course the same attitude from any social institutions such as the church, if they are attached to the government. And if such institutions were to control education, they would seek to indoctrinate submission and conformity by controlling and influencing the teachers, since they would hold the power of reward; the teachers would in turn so mould their pupils that they would grow up to accept

[1] *Correspondence of David Ricardo*, no. 109, Mill to Ricardo, 23 August 1815.

rather than to criticise, to conform and conserve rather than to reform.

It is in this way that it seems to me that the plea against church-controlled education in *Schools for All* may be seen as an illustration of Mill's theory of social and political education. A government which is corrupt influences a social institution, the church, which in turn seeks to control education by controlling the opinions and characters of the teachers. Here is what Mill meant when he said 'the rewards and punishments which society has to bestow . . . are so great, that to adopt the opinions of which it approves, to perform the acts which it admires, to acquire the character, in short, which it "delighteth to honour", can seldom fail to be the leading object of those of whom it is composed. And as this potent influence operates upon those who conduct both the domestic education and the technical, it is next to impossible . . . that it should not fall in with instead of counteracting . . . that which social education produces' (p. 117, below). He is of course making a general point and establishing a general theory, but like all his thinking it is closely linked with his day, and in this case the church and its desire to control education were an exact illustration of what he meant by the indirect influence of a bad government and a bad society through their power over education, on its pupils.

Holding this view of the government and society of his day, one would expect Mill to distrust a national system of education run by the state, particularly since his individualism would predispose him against such collective activity. Yet the stronger desire in Mill's nature was that there should be 'schools for all' and he saw that private charity, even if the religious controversy could be solved, would be hard put to provide this. At about the same time, therefore, we find him writing, albeit reluctantly, in favour of state education:—

And with regard to the danger of training the people generally to habits of servility and toleration of arbitrary power, if their education be entrusted to Government, or persons patronised by the Government,—we can only say, that although we are far from considering the danger either as small or chimerical, it is still so very great and good to have the whole facility of reading and writing diffused through the whole body of the people, that we should be willing to run considerable risks for its acquirement, or even greatly to accelerate that acquirement. There is something in the possession of those keys of knowledge and of thought, so truly admirable, that, when joined to another inestimable blessing, it is scarcely possible for any government to convert them into instruments of evil. That security is—the Liberty of the Press. Let the people only be taught to read, though by instruments ever so little friendly to their general interests, and the very intelligence of the age will provide them with books which will prove an antidote to the poison of their pedagogues . . . But grant . . . a reading people and a free press,—and the prejudices on which misrule supports itself will gradually and silently disappear. The impressions, indeed, which it is possible to make at the early age at which reading and writing are taught, and during the very short time that teaching lasts, are so very slight and transitory, that they must be easily effaced whenever there is anything to counteract them.[1]

This passage seems to me important in several ways. It states that formal education is relatively impotent

[1] *Edinburgh Review*, February 1813, pp. 211–12.

against the power of society: it is interesting that Mill comments on the shortness of the period of formal education, and this by itself would reduce its effect compared with later social influences. But when we look carefully at all his writings on this general point we find him speaking in more than one way. In the essay *Education* he argues that early childhood is important: it is here that the 'primary habits' are formed, and the 'primary habits are the fundamental character of the man'—the 'habits which are then contracted, are the most pervading and operative of them all'. This, by implication, argues that later social influences are unimportant, save in their indirect influence on parents and teachers. And we should notice that one cannot even talk of the *indirect* influence of society via parents and teachers without assuming that their own early education could be nullified by later social influences, which is the reverse of what we have just quoted from the essay. On the other hand, he wrote in his *History of British India*: 'The most efficient part of education is that which is derived from the tone and temper of society . . . which . . . depend altogether upon the laws and the government.'[1] And we have his earlier reference, in his Commonplace Book, to Plato saying the same thing. There seems no doubt that Mill did believe that society and the state were influential, and at times he writes as if they were the ultimate determinants of the character of their members. The only thing which is clear is that the doctrines of social and political education are based not on association psychology, whether mechanical or otherwise, but on psychological hedonism.

[1] Quoted in Stokes, *The English Utilitarians and India* (Oxford, 1959), p. 57.

We may gain some help in deciding what Mill really thought, if we look at an important implication of saying that society and the state were *determinants* of education. This would surely mean a doctrine of the social determination of knowledge—a doctrine which was later to become fashionable. For if these two forces—society and the state—are ultimately all-powerful, how would anyone be free from them; would not thinking be inevitably corrupted by such forces, and would not all thought be relative to and determined by the society in which it took place? In the end such a theory is, of course, self-destructive and circular, for if thought is socially determined, so must that comment about thought be socially determined. And if society exercises such a dominating influence how can we explain the existence of critics, such as Mill himself, of that society?

To ascribe any such view to Mill would be wrong, as is made clear from his commendation of state provision of education which we have quoted. Despite the powers of society and the state, despite the corrupting effect of both in the England of his day, Mill thought universal literacy together with liberty of the press could save the day and advance reform. The importance he attached to the latter is clear from the many entries in his Commonplace Book, and it was the subject of one of his articles for the *Encyclopedia*. But the point of all this is that Mill thought that human reason would ultimately prevail. His faith was in education and free discussion. To produce this, social and political reform must precede, for without them educational reform would have minimal, though not negligible effects. He was not denying the possibility of reform, as is the logical corollary of some of his remarks on social education, or asserting the inevitable corruption of thought, but rather indicating *how* reform must come. And if he were asked how it could ever come if society were all-powerful in its effects, he would have to reply that some might emancipate themselves and ultimately all would be converted by the logic of argument. His ultimate faith, in common with all the utilitarian school, was in the rationality of man.

Utilitarianism, as Dicey and others have shewn, was immensely influential throughout the nineteenth century and we should, in conclusion, consider James Mill's place in the movement and especially the place of his educational theory. Plamenatz has shewn that utilitarianism had a long and continuous intellectual ancestry. I would argue that James Mill should not be regarded, in the main, as the product of this tradition: he was educated outside it, by Scottish philosophers who were its critics, and by his study of Plato and Aristotle. But if he was not the product of a tradition, he, with Bentham, was certainly the founder of utilitarianism as we know it. It was Mill who transformed Bentham's legal theories into a movement and it was Mill also who equipped political utilitarianism with a philosophical basis. This dual quality of the movement is exemplified in this volume, where we have both a philosophy of education and a practical plan for immediate action.

Utilitarianism is distinguished, as we have noted, by its faith in human reason. This seems to me to take two forms. Utilitarianism is rationalist in holding that you could state an ideal, which reason could shew to be good, and which men could then work out the best means of attaining. But it was also rationalist in its faith that, if the ideal were good, *all* men would realise this and work towards it. In this, it stands in sharp contrast to theories which emphasise the irrational motivation of various kinds which in fact brings about political change.

Having this faith that reason would prevail, utilitarianism, one might suppose, stood in more need than most of a philosophy of education; and in assessing Mill's essay *Education* from this point of view, the reader may feel that it takes human rationality too much for granted. To be fair to Mill, he does argue the need for intellectual education for all, and he also argues, quite consistently in terms of his environmentalist psychology, that such intellectual education is possible for all. And wherever he specifies a curriculum, whether for his son, for Francis Place's daughter, or for University College, London, Logic, or the power of correct reasoning, occupies pride of place. Mill himself once wrote to William Allen: 'I am afraid I have expressed myself in favour of my own opinion, with an appearance of warmth, which may induce you to yield more to my *will* than to my *reason*. I beg you will let it have no such effect.'[1] If he did not always live up to this faith, it is fair to say that it was his ideal.

The essay should also be considered not as part of utilitarian thought, but in its own right, as a contribution to educational theory. For it raises, even if it does not satisfactorily resolve, major problems in philosophy of education. From this point of view, there is much to be said for assessing the essay, at some stage in our thinking, in the manner suggested by the late Professor Cavenagh, from whom it is worth quoting at length:

The early chapters of John Stuart Mill's *Autobiography*

[1] Brougham MSS. 10,775. Mill to Allen, 17 January 1811.

form the best introduction to a study of his father's views. For the system there described, though the most amazing ever devised by man, was of a piece with the Benthamite principle that, just as a nation's character is the result of its laws, so the individual character can by education be moulded to any pattern we please. 'In psychology,' says J. S. Mill of his father, 'his fundamental doctrine was the formation of all human character by circumstances, through the universal Principle of Association, and the consequent unlimited possibility of improving the moral and intellectual condition of mankind by education. Of all his doctrines none was more important than this, or needs more to be insisted on; unfortunately there is none which is more contradictory to the prevailing tendencies of speculation, both in his time and since.' As an educational doctrine this was not new. 'I think I may say,' writes Locke at the beginning of his *Thoughts concerning Education*, 'that of all the men we meet with, nine parts of ten are what they are, good or evil, useful or not, by their education.' Helvétius, James Mill's immediate master, exaggerates Locke's postulate of the *tabula rasa*: in his famous chapter 'L'Education peut tout' he asserts definitely that 'l'éducation nous fait ce que nous sommes.' Mill in his article on Education writes rather more cautiously. Just as Robert Owen claims that 'any character, from the best to the worst, from the most ignorant to the most enlightened, may be given *to any community*,' so Mill claims that 'This much, at any rate, is ascertained, that all the difference which exists, or can ever be made to exist, between one *class* of men, and another, is wholly owing to education.'

In these contexts 'education' is of course used in a wide sense; it means in fact 'environment' or 'nurture' as we now distinguish it from 'nature'. But even in the narrower sense of instruction, Mill deliberately set out to educate his son to a pattern; there was a concerted plan between him and Bentham to leave 'the poor boy a successor worthy of both of us'. It is worth while inquiring how far the result bears out the theory that education can accomplish everything. We must first rid our minds of modern sentiments about childhood: it is irrelevant to say that Mill deserved prosecution for cruelty. Nor should we argue that both the Mills were people of abnormal ability; the question is whether John Mill became the sort of man that his father intended. In a sense he did: he undoubtedly carried on his father's work and succeeded him as leader of the Utilitarians; his very special training made him from an early age an acute thinker on logic and political economy. But while he retained many of the Benthamite principles, he changed Utilitarianism as a whole in a way that its originators would not have approved. And these changes arose from the developments in Mill's character which were directly opposed to his early education. Had he been the hard, unemotional, rather unpleasant man that his father was—even Bentham attributed his political opinions less to his love of the many than to his hatred of the few—all would have gone according to plan; on the contrary, though deficient on the sensual, he was more than commonly developed on the emotional side, as is amply proved by his warm friendships and his infatuation for the lady whom he eventually married.

The turning point in Mill's development came, later than with normal adolescents, at the age of twenty; it is minutely described in the chapter 'A Crisis in my Mental History.' After a long spell of overwork he fell into a state of depression—a nervous breakdown, we should probably call it nowadays—in which he discovered that the 'advantage of a quarter of a century over his contemporaries' which his father's training had given him was of no avail. His education had failed to create 'the pleasure of sympathy with human beings, and the feelings which made the good of others, and especially of mankind on a large scale, the object of existence.' In other words, the calculated pursuit of happiness, the foundation of Utilitarianism, had missed 'the greatest and surest sources of happiness.' Further, he lacked what he calls 'the passive susceptibilities,' the whole aesthetic side of life. Beauty made no appeal to James Mill; 'sentimentality' (as he called anything poetical) was his bugbear; and so the whole world of art, as having no connexion with political philosophy, was omitted from his son's training. Hence the poetry of Wordsworth came as a divine revelation to Mill: he had always felt the beauty of natural scenery: he now found a new life in its transfiguration by the poet. Modern psychology has emphasised almost *ad nauseam* the affective side of human nature; but if there be any who still believe in an exclusively rational education they should take warning by John Stuart Mill. Had not nature triumphed over nurture he would either have lost his reason or at any rate have been unable to accomplish the noble work of his later life. Thus even for the specific end that James Mill had in view, to construct a Utilitarian robot, his system failed. Never has an education been more ably directed; it was a test case: education is not all-powerful.

Apart from this general question it is obvious that Mill's training overlooked other sides of human nature. It was entirely bookish: it 'was in itself much more fitted for training me to *know* than to *do*.' Again, in spite of the emphasis laid on physical education in James Mill's article, no room was left for play. His only exercise consisted of walks, during which he gave his father a summary of the books he had been reading. 'I was never a boy,' he said later, 'never played at cricket; it is better to let Nature have her way.' With such a childhood, followed by a sedentary life, it is remarkable that he withstood so long the consumptive tendency of his family. One cannot even entirely agree that 'whatever else it may have done' his education 'proved how much more than is commonly supposed may be taught, and well taught, in those early years which, in the common modes of what is called instruction, are little better than wasted'; for this claim begs the question: it was this very saving of 'waste' that did the damage.

So much for James Mill's educational practice. According to his own principles we shall expect to find his theory correspondingly erroneous; for he was rightly indignant at 'the common expression that something was true in theory but required correction in practice.' Yet it would be quite misleading to suggest that his article is without value; on the contrary it is one of the finest treatises on education in the English language. Its interest is not merely historical, for Mill was in several ways a pioneer. Thus he definitely grounds educational theory on psychology: 'the business is . . . to put the knowledge which we possess respecting the human mind, into that order and form, which is most advantageous for drawing from it the practical rules of education.' We differ from him only that we now realise better the complexity of the human mind; we no longer suppose that it can be made 'as plain as the road from Charing Cross to St. Paul's.' Again, in his insistence on the influence of the body upon the mind, further knowledge has merely confirmed his speculations. It was the first attempt at a completely scientific treatment of education. Macaulay's jibes were not altogether unprovoked: Mill was in a way 'an Aristotelian of the fifteenth century, born out of due season'; his style 'is generally as dry as that of Euclid's Elements.' But in spite of all that, his close reasoning is well worth the effort of following; and a critical examination of his argument is highly instructive.

Superior figures in the texts refer to the Notes which will be found on pp. 194–8.

EDUCATION

Introduction.—Extent of the Subject.—The different Questions which it involves

The end of Education is to render the individual, as much as possible, an instrument of happiness, first to himself, and next to other beings.

The properties, by which he is fitted to become an instrument to this end, are, partly, those of the body, and partly those of the mind.

Happiness depends upon the condition of the body, either immediately, as where the bodily powers are exerted for the attainment of some good; or mediately, through the mind, as where the condition of the body affects the qualities of the mind.

Education, in the sense in which it is usually taken, and in which it shall here be used, denotes the means which may be employed to render the *mind*, as far as possible, an operative cause of happiness. The mode in which the *body* may be rendered the most fit for operating as an instrument of happiness is generally considered as a different species of inquiry; belonging to physicians, and others, who study the means of perfecting the bodily powers.

Education, then, in the sense in which we are now using the term, may be defined, the best employment of all the means which can be made use of, by man, for rendering the human mind to the greatest possible degree the cause of human happiness. Every thing, therefore, which operates, from the first germ of existence, to the final extinction of life, in such a manner as to affect those qualities of the mind on which happiness in any degree depends, comes within the scope of the present inquiry. Not to turn every thing to account is here, if any where, bad economy, in the most emphatical sense of the phrase.

The field, it will easily be seen, is exceedingly comprehensive. It is everywhere, among enlightened men, a subject of the deepest complaint, that the business of education is ill performed; and that, in this, which might have been supposed the most interesting of all human concerns, the practical proceedings are far from corresponding with the progress of the human mind. It may be remarked, that, notwithstanding all that has been written on the subject, even the *theory* of education has not kept pace with philosophy; and it is unhappily true, that the *practice* remains to a prodigious distance behind the theory. One reason why the theory, or the combination of ideas which the present state of knowledge might afford for improving the business of education, remains so imperfect, probably is, that the writers have taken but a partial view of the subject; in other words, the greater number have mistaken a part of it for the whole. And another reason of not less importance is, that they have generally contented themselves with vague ideas of the object or end to which education is required as the means. One grand purpose of the present inquiry will be to obviate all those mistakes; and, if not to exhibit that comprehensive view, which we think is desirable, but to which our limits are wholly inadequate; at any rate, to conduct the reader into that train of thought which will lead him to observe for himself the boundaries of the subject. If a more accurate conception is formed of the end, a better estimate will be made of what is suitable as the means.

1. It has been remarked, that every thing, from the first germ of existence to the final extinction of life, which operates in such a manner as to affect those qualities of the mind on which happiness in any degree depends, comes within the scope of the present inquiry. Those circumstances may be all arranged, according to the hackneyed division, under two heads: They are either physical or moral; meaning by physical, those of a material nature, which operate more immediately upon the material part of the frame; by moral, those of a mental nature, which operate more immediately upon the mental part of the frame.

2. In order to know in what manner things operate upon the mind, it is necessary to know how the mind is constructed. *Quicquid recipitur, recipitur ad modum recipientis.* This is the old aphorism, and nowhere more applicable than to the present case. If you attempt to act upon the mind, in ways not adapted to its nature, the least evil you incur is to lose your labour.

3. As happiness is the end, and the means ought to be nicely adapted to the end, it is necessary to inquire, What are the qualities of mind which chiefly conduce to happiness,—both the happiness of the individual himself, and the happiness of his fellow-creatures?

It appears to us, that this distribution includes the whole of the subject. Each of these divisions branches itself out into a great number of inquiries. And, it is manifest, that the complete development of any one of them would require a greater space than we can allow for the whole. It is, therefore, necessary for us, if we aim at a comprehensive view, to confine ourselves to a skeleton.

The first of these inquiries is the most practical, and,

therefore, likely to be the most interesting. Under the Physical Head, it investigates the mode in which the qualities of the mind are affected by the health, the aliment, the air, the labour, &c. to which the individual is subject. Under the Moral Head it includes what may be called, 1. Domestic Education, or the mode in which the mind of the individual is liable to be formed by the conduct of the individuals composing the family in which he is born and bred: 2. Technical or scholastic education, including all those exercises upon which the individual is put, as means to the acquisition of habits, —habits either conducive to intellectual and moral excellence, or even to the practice of the manual arts: 3. Social education, or the mode in which the mind of the individual is acted upon by the nature of the political institutions under which he lives.

The two latter divisions comprehend what is more purely theoretical; and the discussion of them offers fewer attractions to that class of readers, unhappily numerous, to whom intellectual exercises have not by habit been rendered delightful. The inquiries, however, which are included under these divisions, are required as a foundation to those included under the first. The fact is, that good practice can, in no case, have any solid foundation but in sound theory. This proposition is not more important, than it is certain. For, What is theory? The *whole* of the knowledge, which we possess upon any subject, put into that order and form in which it is most easy to draw from it good practical rules. Let any one examine this definition, article by article, and show us that it fails in a single particular. To recommend the separation of practice from theory is, therefore, simply, to recommend bad practice.

SECTION I

Theory of the Human Mind.—Its Importance in the Doctrine of Education

1. The first, then, of the inquiries, embraced by the great subject of education, is that which regards the nature of the human mind; and the business is, agreeably to the foregoing definition of theory, to put the knowledge which we possess respecting the human mind, into that order and form, which is most advantageous for drawing from it the practical rules of education. The question is, How the mind, with those properties which it possesses, can, through the operation of certain means, be rendered most conducive to a certain end? To answer this question, the whole of its properties must be known. The whole science of human nature is, therefore, but a branch of the science of education. Nor can education assume its most perfect form, till the science of the human mind has reached its highest point of improvement. Even an outline, however, of the philosophy of the human mind would exceed the bounds of the present article; we must, therefore, show what ought to be done, rather than attempt, in any degree, to execute so extensive a project.

With respect to the human mind, as with respect to every thing else, all that passes with us under the name of knowledge is either matter of experience, or, to carry on the analogy of expression, matter of guess. The first is real knowledge; the properties of the object correspond to it. The latter is supposititious knowledge, and the properties of the object do or do not correspond to it; most likely not. The first thing desirable is, to make an exact separation of those two kinds of knowledge; and, as much as possible, to confine ourselves to the first.

What, then, is it which we experience with regard to the human mind? And what is it which we guess? We have experience of ourselves, when we *see*, when we *hear*, when we *taste*, when we *imagine*, when we *fear*, when we *love*, when we *desire*; and so on. And we give names, as above, to distinguish what we experience of ourselves, on one of those occasions, from what we experience on another. We have experience of other men exhibiting *signs* of having similar experiences of themselves, that is, of *seeing*, *hearing*, and so on. It is necessary to explain, shortly, what is here meant by a sign. When we ourselves *see*, *hear*, *imagine*, &c., certain actions of ours commonly follow. We know, accordingly, that if any one, observing those actions, were to infer that we had been *seeing*, *hearing*, &c. the inference would be just. As often then as we observe similar actions in other men, we infer that they, too, have been seeing or hearing; and we thus regard the action as the sign.

Having got names to distinguish the state or experience of ourselves, when we say, *I see*, *I hear*, *I wish*, and so on; we find occasion for a name which will distinguish the having any (be it what it may) of those experiences, from the being altogether without them; and, for this purpose, we say, *I feel*, which will apply, generally, to any of the cases in which we say, *I see*, or *hear*, or *remember*, or *fear*; and comprehends the meaning of them all. The term *I think*, is commonly used for a purpose nearly the same. But it is not quite so comprehensive: there are several things which we should include under the term *our experience of our mind*, to which we should not extend the term *I think*. But there is nothing included under it to which we should not extend the term *I feel*. This is truly, therefore, the generic term.

All our experience, then, of the human mind, is confined to the several occasions on which the term *I feel* can be applied. And, now, What does all this experience amount to? What is the knowledge which it affords? It is, first, a knowledge of the *feelings* themselves; we can remember what, one by one, they were. It is, next, a knowledge of the order in which they follow one another; and this is all. But this description, though a just one, is so very general as to be little instructive. It is not easy, however, to speak about those feelings minutely and correctly; because the language which we must apply to them, is ill adapted to the purpose.

Let us advert to the first branch of this knowledge, that of the feelings themselves. The knowledge of the simple cases, may be regarded as easy; the feeling is distinct at the moment of experience, and is distinctly remembered afterwards. But the difficulty is great with the complex cases. It is found, that a great number of simple feelings are apt to become so closely united, as often to assume the appearance of only one feeling, and to render it extremely difficult to distinguish from one another the simple feelings of which it is composed. And one of the grand questions which divide the philosophers of the present day, is, which feelings are simple, and which are complex. There are two sorts which all have regarded as simple: those which we have when we say, I hear, I see, I feel, I taste, I smell, corresponding to the five senses, and the copies of these sensations, called ideas of sense. Of these, the second take place only in consequence of the first, they are, as it were, a revival of them; not the same feelings with the sensations or impressions on the senses, but feelings which bear a certain resemblance to them. Thus, when a man sees the light of noon, the feeling he has is called an *impression*,—the impression of light; when he shuts his eyes and has a feeling,—the type or relict of the impression,—he is not said to *see* the light, or to have the *impression* of light, but to *conceive* the light, or have an idea of it.

These two,—*impressions*, and their corresponding *ideas*,—are simple feelings, in the opinion of all philosophers. But there is one set of philosophers who think that these are the only simple feelings, and that all the rest are merely combinations of them. There is another class of philosophers who think that there are original feelings beside impressions and ideas; as those which correspond to the words *remember*, *believe*, *judge*, *space*, *time*, &c. Of the first are Hartley[1] and his followers in England, Condillac[2] and his followers in France; of the second description are Dr Reid[3] and his followers in this country, Kant[4] and the German school of metaphysicians in general on the Continent.

It is evident, that the determination of this question with regard to the first branch of inquiry, namely, what the feelings are, is of very great importance with regard to the second branch, namely, what is the order in which those feelings succeed one another. For how can it be known how they succeed one another, if we are ignorant which of them enter into those several groups which form the component parts of the train? It is of vast importance, then, for the business of education, that the analysis of mind should be accurately performed; in other words, that all our complex feelings should be accurately resolved into the simple ones of which they are composed. This, too, is of absolute necessity for the accurate use of language; as the greater number of words are employed to denote those groups of simple feelings which we call complex ideas.

In regard to all events, relating to mind or body, our knowledge extends not beyond two points: The first is, a knowledge of the events themselves; the second is, a knowledge of the order of their succession. The expression in words of the first kind of knowledge is history; the expression of the second is philosophy; and to render that expression short and clear is the ultimate aim of philosophy.

The first steps in ascertaining the order of succession among events are familiar and easy. One occurs, and then another, and after that a third, and so on; but at first it is uncertain whether this order is not merely accidental, and such as may never recur. After a time it is observed, that events, similar to those which have already occurred, are occurring again and again. It is next observed, that they are always followed, too, by the same sort of events by which those events were followed to which they are similar; that these second events are followed, in the third place, by events exactly similar to those which followed the events which they resemble; and that there is, thus, an endless round of the same sequences.

If the order in which one event follows another were always different, we should know events only one by one, and they would be infinitely too numerous to receive names. If we could observe none but very short sequences, if, for example, we could ascertain that one event was, indeed, always followed by one other of the same description, but could not trace any constancy farther, we should thus know events by sequences of twos and twos. But those sequences would also be a great deal too numerous to receive names.

The history of the human mind informs us, that the sequences which are first observed are short ones. They are still, therefore, too numerous to receive names. But men compound the matter. They give names to sequences which they are most interested in observing, and leave the rest unnamed. When they have occasion to speak of the unnamed successions, they apply to them, the best way they can, the names which they have got; endeavouring to make a partial naming answer an universal purpose. And hence almost all the confusion of language and of thought arises.

The great object, then, is, to ascertain sequences more and more extensive, till, at last, the succession of all events may be reduced to a number of sequences sufficiently small for each of them to receive a name; then, and then only, shall we be able to speak wholly free from confusion.

Language affords an instructive example of this mode of ascertaining sequences. In language, the words are the events. When an ignorant man first hears another speak an unknown language, he hears the sounds one by one, but observes no sequence. At last he gathers a knowledge of the use of a few words, and then he has observed a few sequences; and so he goes on till he understands whatever he hears. The sequences, however, which he has observed, are of no greater extent than is necessary to understand the meaning of the speaker; they are, by consequence, very numerous and confusing.

Next comes the grammarian; and he, by dividing the words into different kinds, observes that these kinds follow one another in a certain order, and thus ascertains more enlarged sequences, which, by consequence reduces their number.

Nor is this all; it is afterwards observed, that words consist, some of one syllable, and some of more than one; that all language may thus be resolved into syllables, and that syllables are much less in number than words: that, therefore, the number of sequences in which they can be formed are less in number, and, by consequence, are more extensive. This is another step in tracing to the most comprehensive sequences the order of succession in that class of events wherein language consists.

It is afterwards observed, that these syllables themselves are compounded; and it is at last found, that they may all be resolved into a small number of elementary sounds corresponding to the simple letters. All language is then found to consist of a limited number of sequences, made up of the different combinations of few letters.

It is not pretended that the example of language is exactly parallel to the case which it is brought to illustrate. It is sufficient if it aids the reader in seizing the idea which we mean to convey. It shews the analogy between the analysing of a complex sound, namely, a word, into the simple sounds of which it is composed, to wit, letters; and the analysing of a complex feeling, such as the idea of a rose, into the simple feelings of sight, of touch, of taste, of smell, of which the complex idea or feeling is made up. It affords, also, a proof of the commanding knowledge which is attained of a train of events, by observing the sequences which are formed of the simplest elements into which they can be resolved; and it thus illustrates the two grand operations, by successful perseverance in which the knowledge of the human mind is to be perfected.

It is upon a knowledge of the sequences which take place in the human feelings or thoughts, that the structure of education must be reared. And, though much undoubtedly remains to be cleared up, enough is already known of those sequences to manifest the shameful defects of that education with which our supineness, and love of things as they are, rest perfectly satisfied.

As the happiness, which is the end of education, depends upon the actions of the individual, and as all the actions of man are produced by his feelings or thoughts, the business of education is, to make certain feelings or thoughts take place instead of others. The business of education, then, is to work upon the mental successions. As the sequences among the letters or simple elements of speech, may be made to assume all the differences between nonsense and the most sublime philosophy, so the sequences, in the feelings which constitute human thought, may assume all the differences between the extreme of madness and of wickedness, and the greatest attainable heights of wisdom and virtue: And almost the whole of this is the effect of education. That, at least, all the difference which exists between classes or bodies of men is the effect of education, will, we suppose, without entering into the dispute about individual distinctions, be readily granted; that it is education wholly which constitutes the remarkable difference between the Turk and the Englishman, and even the still more remarkable difference between the most cultivated European and the wildest savage. Whatever is made of any *class* of men, we may then be sure is possible to be made of the whole human race. What a field for exertion! What a prize to be won!

Mr Hobbs,[5] who saw so much further into the texture of human thought than all who had gone before him, was the first man, as far as we remember, who pointed out (what is peculiarly *knowledge* in this respect) the order in which our feelings succeed one another, as a distinct object of study. He marked, with sufficient clearness, the existence, and the cause of the sequences; but, after a very slight attempt to trace them, he diverged to other inquiries, which had this but indirectly for their object.

'The succession,' he says (*Human Nature*, ch. 4) 'of conceptions, in the mind, series or consequence' (by *consequence* he means *sequence*) 'of one after another, may be casual and incoherent, as in dreams, for the most part; and it may be orderly, as when the former thought introduceth the latter. The cause of the coherence or consequence (*sequence*) of one conception to another, is their first coherence or consequence at that time when they are produced by sense; as, for example, from St Andrew the mind runneth to St Peter, because their names are read together; from St Peter to a stone, for the same cause; from stone to foundation, because we see them together; and, according to this example, the mind may run almost from any thing to any thing. But, as in the sense, the conception of cause and effect may succeed one another, so may they, *after* sense, in the imagination.' By the succession in the *imagination* it is evident he means the succession of *ideas*, as by the succession in *sense* he means the succession of sensations.

Having said that the conceptions of *cause* and *effect* may succeed one another in the sense, and after sense in the imagination, he adds, 'And, for the most part, they do so; the cause whereof is the appetite of them who, having a conception of the *end*, have next unto it a conception of the next *means* to that end; as when a man from a thought of honour, to which he hath an appetite, cometh to the thought of wisdom, which is the next means thereunto; and from thence to the thought of study, which is the next means to wisdom.' (Ib.) Here is a declaration with respect to three grand laws in the sequence of our thoughts. The first is, that the succession of ideas follows the same order which takes place in that of the impressions. The second is, that the order of cause and effect is the most common order in the successions in the imagination, that is in the succession of ideas. And the third is, that the appetites of individuals have a great power over the successions of ideas; as the thought of the object which the individual desires, leads him to the thought of that by which he may attain it.

Mr Locke[6] took notice of the sequence in the train of ideas, or the order in which they follow one another, only for a particular purpose;—to explain the intellectual singularities which distinguish particular men. 'Some of our ideas,' he says, 'have a natural correspondence and connection one with another. It is the office and excellence of our reason to trace these, and hold them together in that union and correspondence which is founded in their peculiar beings. Besides this, there is another connexion of ideas, wholly owing to chance or custom; ideas that are not at all of kin come to be so united in some men's minds, that it is very hard to separate them; they always keep in company, and the one no sooner at any time comes into the understanding, but its associate appears with it; and if they are more than two which are thus united, the whole gang, always inseparable, show themselves together.' There is no attempt here to trace the order of sequence, or to ascertain which antecedents are followed by which consequents; and the accidental, rather than the more general phenomena, are those which seem particularly to have struck his attention. He gave, however, a name to the matter of fact. When one idea is regularly followed by another, he called this constancy of conjunction *the association of the ideas*; and this is the name by which, since the time of Locke, it has been commonly distinguished.

Mr Hume[7] perceived much more distinctly than any of the philosophers who had gone before him, that to philosophize concerning the human mind, was to trace the order of succession among the elementary feelings of the man. He pointed out three great laws or comprehensive sequences, which he thought included the whole. Ideas followed one another, he said, according to *resemblance*, *contiguity* in time and place, and *cause and effect*. The last of these, the sequence according to cause and effect, was very distinctly conceived, and even the cause of it explained by Mr Hobbs. That of contiguity in time and place is thus satisfactorily explained by Mr Hume. 'It is evident,' he says, 'that as the senses, in changing their objects, are necessitated to change them regularly, and take them as they lie contiguous to each other, the imagination must, by long custom, acquire the same method of thinking, and run along the parts of space and time in conceiving its objects.' (*Treatise of Human Nature*, P. 1. B. 1. sect. 4.) This is a reference to one of the laws pointed out by Hobbs, namely, that the order of succession among the ideas, follows the order that took place among the impressions. Mr Hume shows, that the order of sense is much governed by contiguity, and why; and assigns this as a sufficient reason of the order which takes place in the imagination. Of the next sequence, that according to resemblance, he gives no account, and only appeals to the consciousness of his reader for the existence of the fact. Mr Hume farther remarked, that what are called our complex ideas, are only a particular class of cases belonging to the same law—the law of the succession of ideas; every complex idea being only a certain number of simple ideas, which succeed each other so rapidly, as not to be separately distinguished without an effort of thought. This was a great discovery; but it must at the same time be owned, that it was very imperfectly developed by Mr Hume. That philosopher proceeded, by aid of these principles, to account for the various phenomena of the human mind. But though he made some brilliant developements, it is nevertheless true, that he did not advance very far in the general object. He was misled by the pursuit of a few surprising and paradoxical results, and when he had arrived at them he stopped.

After him, and at a short interval, appeared two philosophers, who were more sober-minded, and had better aims. These were Condillac and Hartley. The first work of Condillac appeared some years before the publication of that of Hartley; but the whole of Hartley's train of thought has so much the air of being his own, that there is abundant reason to believe the speculations of both philosophers equally original. They both began upon the ground that all simple ideas are copies of impressions; that all complex ideas are only simple ideas united by the principle of association. They proceeded to examine all the phenomena of the human mind, and were of opinion that the principle of association, or the succession of one simple idea after another, according to certain laws, accounts for the whole; that these laws might, by meditation, be ascertained and applied; and that then the human mind would be understood, as far as man has the means of knowing it.

The merit of Condillac is very great. It may yet, perhaps, be truer to say, that he wrote admirably upon philosophy, than that he was a great philosopher. His power consists in expression; he conveys metaphysical ideas with a union of brevity and clearness which never has been surpassed. But though he professed rather to deliver the opinions of others, than to aim at invention, it cannot be denied that he left the science of the human mind in a much better state than he found it; and this is equivalent to discovery. As a teacher, in giving, in this field, a right turn to the speculations of his countrymen, his value is incalculable; and there is, perhaps, no one human being, with the exception of Locke, who was his master, to whom, in this respect, the progress of the human mind is more largely indebted. It is also true, that to form the conception of tracing the sequences among our simple ideas, as comprehending the whole of the philosophy of the human mind, even with the helps which Hume had afforded, and it is more than probable that neither Condillac nor Hartley had ever heard of a work which, according to its author, had fallen deadborn from the press, was philosophical and sagacious in the highest degree.

It must be allowed, however, that, in expounding the various mental phenomena, Condillac does not display the same penetration and force of mind, or the same comprehensiveness, as Dr Hartley. He made great *progress* in showing how those phenomena might be resolved into the sequences of simple ideas; but Dr Hartley made still greater. We do not mean to pronounce a positive opinion either for or against the grand undertaking of Dr Hartley, to resolve the whole of the mental phenomena of man into sequences of impressions, and the simple ideas which are the copies of them. But we have no hesitation in saying, that he philosophizes with extraordinary power and sagacity; and it is astonishing how many of the mental phenomena he has clearly resolved; how little, in truth, he has left about which any doubt can remain.

We cannot afford to pursue this subject any farther. This much is ascertained,—that the character of the human mind consists in the sequences of its ideas; that the object of education, therefore, is, to provide for the constant production of certain sequences, rather than others; that we cannot be sure of adopting the best means to that end, unless we have the greatest knowledge of the sequences themselves.

In what has been already ascertained on this subject, we have seen that there are two things which have a wonderful power over those sequences. They are, Custom; and Pain and Pleasure. These are the grand instruments or powers, by the use of which, the purposes of education are to be attained.

Where one idea has followed another a certain number of times, the appearance of the first in the mind is sure to be followed by that of the second, and so on. One of the grand points, then, in the study of education, is to find the means of making, in the most perfect manner, those repetitions on which the beneficial sequences depend.

When we speak of making one idea follow another, and always that which makes part of a good train, instead of one that makes part of a bad train, there is one difficulty; that each idea, taken singly by itself, is as fit to be a part of a bad train as of a good one; for good trains and bad trains are both made out of the same simple elements. Trains, however, take place by sequences of twos, or threes, or any greater number; and the nature of these sequences, as complex parts of a still greater whole, is that which renders the train either salutary or hurtful. Custom is, therefore, to be directed to two points; first to form those sequences, which make the component parts of a good train; and secondly, to join those sequences together, so as to constitute the trains.

When we speak of making one idea follow another, there must always be a starting point; there must be some one idea from which the train begins to flow; and it is pretty evident that much will depend upon this idea. One grand question, then, is, 'What are the ideas which most frequently operate as the commencement of trains?' Knowing what are the ideas which play this important part, we may attach to them by custom, such trains as are the most beneficent. It has been observed that most, if not all, of our trains, start from a sensation, or some impression upon the external or internal nerves. The question then is, which are those sensations, or aggregates of sensations, which are of the most frequent recurrence? it being obviously of importance, that those which give occasion to the greatest number of trains, should be made, if possible, to give occasion only to the best trains. Now the sensations, or aggregates of sensations, which occur in the ordinary business of life, are those of most frequent recurrence; and from which it is of the greatest importance that beneficial trains should commence. Rising up in the morning, and going to bed at night, are aggregates of this description, common to all mankind; so are the commencement and termination of meals. The practical sagacity of priests, even in the rudest ages of the world, perceived the importance, for giving religious trains an ascendancy in the mind, of uniting them, by early and steady custom, with those perpetually recurring sensations. The morning and evening prayers, the grace before and after meals, have something correspondent to them in the religion of, perhaps, all nations.

It may appear, even from these few reflections and illustrations, that, if the sensations, which are most apt to give commencement to trains of ideas, are skilfully selected, and the trains which lead most surely to the happiness, first of the individual himself, and next of his fellow-creatures, are by custom effectually united with them, a provision of unspeakable importance is made for the happiness of the race.

Beside custom, it was remarked by Hobbs, that appetite had a great power over the mental trains. But appetite is the feeling toward pleasure or pain in prospect; that is, future pleasure or pain. To say that appetite, therefore, has power over the mental trains, is to say, that the prospect of pleasure or pain has. That this is true, every man knows by his own experience. The best means, then, of applying the prospect of pleasure and pain to render beneficent trains perpetual in the mind, is the discovery to be made, and to be recommended to mankind.

The way in which pleasure and pain affect the trains of the mind is, as ends. As a train commences in some present sensation, so it may be conceived as terminating in the idea of some future pleasure or pain. The intermediate ideas, between the commencement and the end, may be either of the beneficent description or the hurtful. Suppose the sight of a fine equipage to be the commencement, and the riches which afford it, the appetite, or the end of a train, in the mind of two individuals at the same time. The intermediate ideas in the mind of the one may be beneficent, in the other hurtful. The mind of the one immediately runs over all the honourable and useful modes of acquiring riches, the acquisition of the most rare and useful qualities, the eager watch of all the best opportunities of bringing them into action, and the steady industry with which they may be applied. That of the other recurs to none but the vicious modes of acquiring riches—by lucky accidents, the arts of the adventurer and impostor, by rapine and plunder, perhaps on the largest scale, by all the honours and glories of war. Suppose the one of these trains to be habitual among individuals, the other not: What a difference for mankind!

It is unnecessary to adduce farther instances for the elucidation of this part of our mental constitution. What, in this portion of the field, requires to be done for the science of education, appears to be, First, to ascertain, what are the ends, the really ultimate objects of human desire; Next, what are the most beneficent means of attaining those objects; and Lastly, to accustom the mind to fill up the intermediate space between the present sensation and the ultimate object, with nothing but the ideas of those beneficent means. We are perfectly aware that these instructions are far too general. But we hope it will be carried in mind, that little beyond the most general ideas can be embraced in so confined a sketch; and we are not without an expectation that, such as they are, these expositions will not be wholly without their use.

SECTION II

Qualities of Mind, to the Production of which the Business of Education should be directed

We come now to the second branch of the science of education, or the inquiry what are the qualities with which it is of most importance that the mind of the individual should be endowed. This inquiry we are in hopes the preceding exposition will enable us very materially to abridge. In one sense, it might undoubtedly be affirmed, that all the desirable qualities of the human mind are included in those beneficent sequences of which we have spoken above. But, as it would require, to make this sufficiently intelligible, a more extensive exposition than we are able to afford, we must content ourselves with the ordinary language, and with a more familiar mode of considering the subject.

That intelligence is one of the qualities in question will not be denied, and may speedily be made to appear. To attain happiness is the object: and, to attain it in the greatest possible degree, all the means to that end, which the compass of nature affords, must be employed in the most perfect possible manner. But all the means which the compass of nature, or the system in which we are placed, affords, can only be known by the most perfect knowledge of that system. The highest measure of knowledge is therefore required. But mere knowledge is not enough; a mere magazine of remembered facts is an useless treasure. Amid the vast variety of known things, there is needed a power of choosing, a power of discerning which of them are conducive, which not, to the ends we have in view. The ingredients of intelligence are two, knowledge and sagacity; the one affording the materials upon which the other is to be exerted; the one, showing what exists; the other, converting it to the greatest use; the one, bringing within our ken what is capable, and what is not capable of being used as means; the other, seizing and combining, at the proper moment, whatever is fittest as means to each particular end. This union, then, of copiousness and energy; this possession of numerous ideas, with the masterly command of them, is one of the more immediate ends to which the business of education is to be directed.

With a view to happiness as the end, another quality will easily present itself as indispensable. Conceive that a man knows the materials which can be employed as means, and is prompt and unerring in the mode of combining them; all this power is lost, if there is anything in his nature which prevents him from using it. If he has any appetite in his nature which leads him to pursue certain things with which the most effectual pursuit of happiness is inconsistent, so far this evil is incurred. A perfect command, then, over a man's appetites and desires; the power of restraining them whenever they lead in a hurtful direction; that possession of himself which insures his judgement against the illusions of the passions, and enables him to pursue constantly what he deliberately approves, is indispensably requisite to enable him to produce the greatest possible quantity of happiness. This is what the ancient philosophers called temperance; not exactly the same with what is called the virtue or grace of temperance, in theological morality, which includes a certain portion (in the doctrines of some theological instructors, a very large portion) of abstinence, and not only of abstinence, or the gratuitous renunciation of pleasure, but of the infliction of voluntary pain. This is done with a view to please the God, or object of worship, and to provide, through his favour, for the happiness of a second, or future life. The temperance of the ancient philosophers had a view only to the happiness of the present life, and consisted in the power of resisting the immediate propensity, if yielding to it would lead to an overbalance of evil or prevent the enjoyment of a superior good, in whatever the good or evil of the present life consists. This resisting power consists of two parts; the power of resisting pleasure, and that of resisting pain, the last of which has an appropriate name, and is called Fortitude.

These two qualities, the intelligence which can always choose the best possible means, and the strength which overcomes the misguiding propensities, appear to be sufficient for the happiness of the individual himself; to the pursuit of which it cannot be doubted that he always has sufficient motives. But education, we have said, should be an instrument to render the individual the best possible artificer of happiness, not to himself alone, but also to others. What, then, are the qualities with which he ought to be endowed, to make him produce the greatest possible quantity of happiness to others?

It is evident enough to see what is the first grand division. A man can affect the happiness of others, either by abstaining from doing them harm, or by doing them positive good. To abstain from doing them harm, receives the name of Justice; to do positive good receives that of Generosity. Justice and generosity, then, are the two qualities by which man is fitted to promote the happiness of his fellow-creatures. And it thus appears, that the four cardinal virtues of the ancients do pretty completely include all the qualities, to the possession of which it is desirable that the human mind should be trained. The defect, however, of this description is, that it is far too general. It is evident that the train of mental events which conduct to the proposed results must be far more particularized to insure, in any considerable degree, the effects of instruction; and it must be confessed that the ethical instructions of the ancients failed by remaining too much in generals. What is wanting is, that the incidents of human life should be skilfully classified; both those on the occasion of which they who are the objects of the good acts are pointed out for the receipt of them, and those on the occasion of which they who are to be the instruments are called upon for the performance. It thus appears that the science of Ethics, as well as the science of Intellectuals, must be carried to perfection, before the best foundation is obtained for the science of Education.

SECTION III

Happiness, the End to which Education is devoted.—Wherein it consists, not yet determined

We have spoken of the qualities which are subservient to human happiness, as means to an end. But, before means can be skilfully adapted to an end, the end must be accurately known. To know how the human mind is to be trained to the promotion of happiness, another inquiry then, is necessary; Wherein does human happiness consist? This is a controverted question; and we have introduced it rather with a view to show the place which it occupies in the theory of education, than that we have it in our power to elucidate a subject about which there is so much diversity of opinion, and which some of the disputants lead into very subtle and intricate inquiries. The importance of the question is sufficiently evident from this, that it is the grand central point, to which all other questions and inquiries converge; that point, by their bearing upon which, the value of all other things is determined. That it should remain itself undetermined, implies, that this branch of philosophy is yet far from its highest point of perfection.

The speculation on this subject, too, may be divided into two great classes;[8] that of those who trace up all the elements of happiness, as they do all those of intellect, to the simple sensations which, by their transformation into ideas, and afterwards into various combinations, compose, they think, all the intellectual and moral phenomena of our nature; another, that of those who are not satisfied with this humble origin, who affirm that there is something in human happiness, and in the human intellect, which soars high above this corporeal level; that there are intellectual as well as moral forms, the resplendent objects of human desire, which can by no means be resolved into the grosser elements of sense. These philosophers speak of eternal and immutable truths; truths which are altogether independent of our limited experience; which are truly universal; which the mind recognizes without the aid of the senses; and which are the objects of pure intellect. They affirm, also, that there is a notion of right and of wrong wholly underived from human experience, and independent of the laws which regulate, in this world, the happiness and misery of human life; a right and wrong, the distinction between which is perceived, according to some, by a peculiar sense; according to others, by the faculty which discerns pure truth; according to others, by common sense; it is the same, according to some, with the notion of the fitness and unfitness of things; according to others, with the law of nature; according to others with truth; and there is one eminent philosopher who makes it depend upon sympathy, without determining very clearly whether sympathy depends upon the senses or not.

We cannot too earnestly exhort philosophers to perfect this inquiry; that we may understand at last, not by vague abstract terms, but clearly and precisely, what are the simple ideas included under the term happiness; and what is the real object to which education is pointed; since it is utterly impossible, while there is any vagueness and uncertainty with respect to the end, that there should be the greatest precision and certainty in combining the means.

SECTION IV

Instruments, and practical Expedients, of Education

We come at last to the consideration of the means which are at the disposal of man for endowing the human mind with the qualities on which the generation of happiness depends. Under this head the discussion of the practical expedients chiefly occurs; but it also embraces some points of theory. The degree in which the useful qualities of human nature are, or are not, under the powers of education, is one of the most important.

This is the subject of a famous controversy, with names of the highest authority on both sides of the question. Helvétius, it is true, stands almost alone, on one side.[9] But Helvétius, alone, is a host. No one man, perhaps, has done so much towards perfecting the *theory* of education as Mons. Helvétius; and his books are pregnant with information of the highest importance. Whoever wishes to understand the groundwork of education, can do nothing more conducive to his end, than to study profoundly the expositions of this philosophical inquirer, whether he adopts his conclusions, in all their latitude, or not. That Helvétius was not more admired in his own country, is owing really to the value of his work. It was too solid, for the frivolous taste of the gay circles of Paris, assemblies of pampered noblesse, who wished for nothing but amusement. That he has been so little valued, in this country, is, it must be confessed, owing a little to the same cause; but another has concurred. An opinion has prevailed, a false one, that Helvétius is a peculiarly dangerous enemy to religion; and this has deterred people from reading him; or rather the old people who do not read, have deterred the young who do. There is no book, the author of which does not disguise his unbelief, that can be read with more safety to religion. The author attacks nothing but priestcraft, and in one of the worst of its forms; the popish priestcraft of the dark and middle ages; the idea of which we are well accustomed, in this country, to separate from that of religion. When his phraseology at any time extends, and that is not often, to Christianity itself, or to religion in the abstract, there is nothing calculated to seduce. There is nothing epigrammatic, and sparkling in the expression; nothing sophistical and artfully veiled in the reasoning; a plain proposition is stated, with a plain indication of its evidence; and if your judgement is not convinced, you are not deluded through the fancy.

M. Helvétius says, that if you take men who bring into the world with them the original constituents of their nature, their mental and bodily frame, in that ordinary state of goodness which is common to the great body of mankind,—leaving out of the account the comparatively small number of individuals who come into the world imperfect, and manifestly below the ordinary standard,—you may regard the whole of this great mass of mankind, as equally susceptible of mental excellence; and may trace the causes which make them to differ. If this be so, the power of education embraces every thing between the lowest stage of intellectual and moral rudeness, and the highest state, not only of actual, but of possible perfection. And if the power of education be so immense, the motive for perfecting it is great beyond expression.

The conclusions of Helvétius were controverted directly by Rousseau;[10] and defended, against the strictures of that writer, by the author himself. We recollect few writers in this country who have embraced them.* But our authors have contented themselves, rather with rejecting, than disproving; and, at best, have supported their rejection only by some incidental reflection, or the indication of a discrepancy between his conclusions and theirs.

One of the causes, why people have been so much startled, by the extent to which Helvétius has carried

* There is one brilliant authority on the side of Helvetius: 'It was a favourite opinion of Sir Wm. Jones, that all men are born with an equal capacity of improvement.'—Lord Teignmouth's *Life of Sir William Jones*, vol. ii, p. 211.[11]

the dominion of education, seems to us to be their not including in it nearly so much as he does. They include in it little more than what is expressed by the term schooling; commencing about six or seven years of age, and ending at latest with the arrival of manhood. If this alone is meant by education, it is no doubt true, that education is far indeed from being all-powerful. But if in education is included every thing, which acts upon the being as it comes from the hand of nature, in such a manner as to modify the mind, to render the train of feelings different from what it would otherwise have been; the question is worthy of the most profound consideration. It is probable, that people in general form a very inadequate conception of all the circumstances which act during the first months, perhaps the first moments, of existence, and of the power of those circumstances in giving permanent qualities to the mind. The works of Helvétius would have been invaluable, if they had done nothing more than prove the vast importance of these circumstances, and direct towards them the attention of mankind. Rousseau began this important branch of the study of education. He remarked a variety of important facts, which, till his time, had been almost universally neglected, in the minds of infants, and how much might be done, by those who surround them, to give good or bad qualities to their minds, long before the time at which it had been supposed that education could commence. But Helvétius treated the subject much more profoundly and systematically. He traced the circumstances to the very moment of birth; he showed at how early an age indelible characters may be impressed; nay, that some of the circumstances over which man has a control (for he speaks not of others), circumstances on which effects of the greatest importance depend, may be traced beyond the birth.

It is evident how much it imports the science of education, that these circumstances should, by careful and continued observation, be all ascertained, and placed in the order best adapted for drawing from them the most efficient practical rules. This is of more importance than determining the question, whether the prodigious difference, which exists among men ordinarily well organized, is owing wholly to the circumstances which have operated upon them since the first moment of their sensitive existence, or is in part produced by original peculiarities. Enough is ascertained to prove, beyond a doubt, that if education does not perform every thing, there is hardly anything which it does not perform: that nothing can be more fatal than the error of those who relax in the vigilance of education, because nature is powerful, and either renders it impossible for them to accomplish much, or accomplishes a great deal without them: that the feeling is much more conformable to experience, and much more conformable to utility, which ascribes every thing to education, and thus carries the motive for vigilance and industry, in that great concern, to its highest pitch. This much, at any rate, is ascertained, that all the difference which exists, or can ever be made to exist, between one *class* of men, and another, is wholly owing to education. Those peculiarities, if any such there be, which sink a man below, or elevate him above the ordinary state of aptitude to profit by education, have no operation in the case of large numbers, or bodies. But large numbers or bodies of men are raised to a high degree of mental excellence; and might, without doubt, be raised to still higher. Other large bodies, or whole nations, have been found in so very low a mental state, as to be little above the brutes. All this vast distance is undeniably the effect of education. This much, therefore, may be affirmed on the side of Helvétius, that a prodigious difference is produced by education; while, on the other hand, it is rather assumed than proved, that any difference exists, but that which difference of education creates.

Circumstances of the Physical Kind which operate upon the Mind in the way of Education

The circumstances which are included under the term Education, in the comprehensive sense in which we have defined it, may be divided, we have said, into Physical, and Moral. We shall now consider the two classes in the order in which we have named them; and have here again to remind the reader, that we are limited to the task of pointing out what we should wish to be done, rather than permitted to attempt the performance.

Three things are desirable with regard to the physical circumstances which operate in the way of education favourably or unfavourably; to collect them fully; to appreciate them duly; and to place them in the order which is most favourable for drawing from them practical rules.

This is a service (common to the sciences of education and mind) which has been very imperfectly rendered. It has been chiefly reserved to medical men to observe the physical circumstances which affect the body and mind of man; but of medical men few have been much skilled in the observation of mental phenomena, or have thought themselves called upon to mark the share which physical circumstances had in producing them. There are indeed some, and those remarkable, exceptions. There is Dr Darwin in our own country,[12] and M. Cabanis in France.[13] They have both of them taken the mind as a part at least of their study; and we are highly indebted to them for the number and value of their observations. They are both philosophers, in the most important sense of the word; they both observed nature for themselves, observed her attentively, and with their view steadily directed to the proper end. But still it is not safe to rely upon them as guides. They were in too great a haste to establish conclusions; and were apt to let their belief run before their evidence. They were not sufficiently careful to distinguish between the different degrees of evidence, and to mark what is required to constitute proof. To do this steadily seems, indeed, to be one of the rarest of all endowments; and was much less the characteristic of the two philosophers we have named, than a wide range of knowledge, from which they collected the facts, and great ingenuity in combining and applying them. Dr Darwin was the most remarkable, both for the strength and the weakness of which we speak. The work of Darwin, to which we chiefly allude, is the *Zoönomia*; though important remarks to the same effect are scattered in his other publications. Cabanis entitled his great work, *Rapports du Physique et du Moral de l'Homme*. And there are some works recently announced by German physiologists, the titles of which promise aids in the same endeavour. But though we expect from them new facts, and ingenious hints, we have less hope of any great number of sound conclusions.

There are certain general names already in use, including the greater number of the physical circumstances which operate in the way of education upon the mind. It will be convenient, because of their commonness, to make use of them on the present occasion, though neither the enumeration which they make is complete, nor the distribution logical.

All the physical circumstances which operate upon the mind are either, 1. inherent in the body; or, 2. external to the body. Those which are external to the body, operate upon the mind, by first operating upon the body.

Of the first kind, the more remarkable seem to be healthiness or sickliness, strength or weakness, beauty or deformity, the temperament, the age, the sex.

Of the second sort, the more remarkable seem to be the aliment, the labour, the air, temperature, action, rest.

Previous to the inquiry concerning the power which physical circumstances exert in the formation of the mind, it may seem that we ought to determine the speculative question respecting the nature of the mind: that is, whether the phenomena of mind may possibly result from a certain organization of matter; or whether something of a different kind, and which we call spiritual, must not be conceived, as the source and organ of thought. We do not mean to enter into this controversy, which would detain us too long. It is not, in the least degree, necessary, for the end which we have in view. Whether the one hypothesis, with respect to the mind, be adopted, or the other, the distribution of the circumstances, which operate in the formation of human character, into those commonly called Physical, and those commonly called Moral, will be as convenient as any distribution which the present state of our knowledge enables us to make; and all that inquiry can do, in regard to those circumstances, is, to trace them accurately, and to observe their effects; that is, to ascertain what they are, and what the order of the mental events by which they are followed. This is simply matter of experience, and what we experience is the same, whether we adopt one opinion, or another, with regard to the nature of that which thinks. It is in what we experience, all ascertained, and put into the best possible shape for ease of comprehension, and ready application to practice, that all useful knowledge on this, as on all other subjects, consists.

1. First, we are to consider the circumstances of the body which have an effect upon the mental sequences. The object is, to ascertain which have a tendency to introduce those sequences which are favourable, which to introduce those that are unfavourable, to human happiness, and how to turn this knowledge to account.

Health and sickness, or the states of body which those names most peculiarly express, are the first of the circumstances which we have enumerated under this head. That these states have a tendency to introduce very different trains of thought, is matter of vulgar experience; but very little has been done to examine such trains, and to ascertain what in each is favourable, and what is unfavourable to human happiness.

We have already seen, that the trains which are favourable to Intelligence, Temperance, Justice, and Generosity, are the trains favourable to human happiness. Now, with respect to Intelligence, it will be seen, that Health is partly favourable, and partly unfavourable; and the same is the case with Sickness. Health is favourable, by allowing that time to be given to study, which many kinds of sickness withdraw, and by admitting a more vigorous attention, which the pain and languor of sickness often impair. It is unfavourable, by introducing that flow of pleasurable ideas which is called high spirits, adverse at a certain pitch to the application of attention; and by leading to that passionate pursuit of pleasure, which diminishes, if it does not destroy, the time for study. The mode in which disease operates upon the mental sequences is a subject of great complexity, and in which little has yet been done to mark distinctly the events, and ascertain the order of their succession. Cabanis, in his seventh memoir, entitled, *De l'Influence des Maladies sur la Formation des Idées et des Affections Morales*, has made a useful beginning toward the elucidation of this subject; but here, as elsewhere, he is too often general and vague. Instruction may also be gleaned from Darwin; but the facts which bear upon this point rather drop from him incidentally, than are anywhere put together systematically for its elucidation. As they were both physicians, however, of great experience, and of unusual skill in the observation of mental phenomena, their opinions are entitled to the greatest respect. The result of the matter is, that an improved medicine is no trifling branch of the art and science of education. Cabanis, accordingly concludes his memoir with the two following propositions:

'1mo. L'état de maladie influe d'une manière directe sur la formation des idées et des affections morales: nous avons même pu montrer dans quelques observations particulières, comment cette influence s'exerce.

'2do. L'observation et l'expérience nous ayant fait decouvrir les moyens de combattre assez souvent avec succés l'état de maladie, l'art qui met en usage ces moyens, peut donc modifier et perfectionner les opérations de l'intelligence et les habitudes de la volonté.'

As it is chiefly through the nervous system, and the centre of that system, the brain, that the mental sequences are affected, and as all the sensitive parts have not an action equally strong, nor equally direct, upon the nerves and brain, diseases affect the mental sequences differently, according to the parts which they invade. The system of the nerves and brain is itself subject to different states of disease. Classified with regard to the functions which that system performs, as the organ of sensibility and of action, these states are thus described by M. Cabanis: '1. Excess of sensibility to all impressions on the one part; excessive action on the organs of motion on the other. 2. Unfitness to receive impressions, in sufficient number, or with the due degree of energy; and a diminution of the activity necessary for the production of the motions. 3. A general disturbance of the functions of the system, without any remarkable appearance of either excess or defect. 4. A bad distribution of the cerebral virtue, either when it exerts itself unequally in regard to time, having fits of extraordinary activity, followed by others of considerable remission; or when it is supplied in wrong proportion to the different organs, of which some are to a great degree abandoned, while there appears in others a concentration of sensibility, and of the excitations or powers by which the movements are affected.'

The effects upon the mental sequences are represented in the following general sketch, which has the advantage of being tolerably comprehensive, though it is unhappily both vague and confused: 'We may lay it down as a general fact, that, in all the marked affections of the nerves, irregularities, less or greater, take place, relative both to the mode in which impressions are received, and to the mode in which the determinations, automatic or voluntary, are formed. On one part, the sensations vary incessantly and rapidly with respect to their vivacity, their energy, and even their number; on another, the strength, the readiness, the facility of action exhibit the greatest inequalities. Hence perpetual fluctuation, from great excitement to languor, from elevation to dejection; a temper and passions variable in the highest degree. In this condition, the mind is always easily pushed to extremes. Either the man has many ideas, with great mental activity and acuteness; or, he is, on the contrary, almost incapable of thinking. It has been well observed, that hypochondriacal persons are by turns both courageous and cowardly; and as the impressions are habitually faulty either by excess or defect, in regard to almost all objects, it is seldom that the images correspond to the reality of things; that the desires and the will obtain the proper force and direction. If, along with these irregularities, which arise from the nervous system, should be found a weakness of the muscular organs, or of some important viscus, as, for example, of the stomach,—the phenomena, though still analogous in the main, will be distinguished by remarkable peculiarities. During the interval of languor, the debility of the muscles renders the sense of weakness, the fainting and drooping, still more complete and oppressive; life appears ready to escape at every instant. The passions are gloomy, excited by trifles, selfish; the ideas are petty, narrow, and bear only upon the objects of the slightest sensations. At the times of excitation, which arrive the more suddenly the greater the weakness; the muscular determinations do not obey the impulses of the brain, unless by starts, which have neither energy nor duration. These impulses serve only to convince the patient more profoundly of his real imbecility; they give him only a feeling of impatience, of discontent, and anxiety. Desires, often sufficiently keen, but commonly repressed by the habitual feeling of weakness, still more increase the discouraging impression. As the peculiar organ of thought cannot act without the concurrence of several others, and as, at that moment, it partakes in some degree of the weakness which affects the organs of movement, the ideas present themselves in crowds; they spring up, but do not arrange themselves in order; the necessary attention is not enjoyed; the consequence is, that this activity of the imagination, which we might expect to afford some compensation for the absence of other faculties, becomes a new source of dejection and despair.'

In this passage, the mental sequences which particular states of disease introduce are clearly shown to have a prodigious influence upon human happiness; but the effects which are produced in respect to intelligence, temperance, generosity and justice, are mixed up together; and the author rather shows how much this subject deserves to be studied, than gives us information from which any considerable degree of practical utility can be derived. The connexion between particular states of body, and particular mental trains, ought to be carefully watched and recorded. When the events, one by one, are accurately distinguished, and made easy to be recognized, and when the order in which they follow one another is known, our power over the trains of those events, power to prevent such as are unfavourable, to produce such as are favourable, to human happiness, will then be at its height; and how to take care of his health will be one of the leading parts of the moral and intellectual education of man.

The state of the body, with regard to health and

disease, is the inherent circumstance of the greatest importance, and we must pass over the rest with a cursory notice. The next we mentioned, are, Strength and Weakness, meaning chiefly muscular strength and weakness; and the natural, habitual, not the accidental, or diseased, state. It is a common observation, that muscular strength is apt to withdraw the owner from mental pursuits, and engage him in such as are more of the animal kind; the acquisition and display of physical powers. Few men of great bodily powers have been much distinguished for mental excellence; some of the greatest ornaments of human nature have been remarkable for bodily weakness. Muscular strength is liable to operate unfavourably upon the moral as well as the intellectual trains of thought. It diminishes that respect for other men, which is so necessary to resist the impulses of passion; it presents innumerable occasions for playing the tyrant with impunity; and fosters, therefore, all that train of ideas, in which the tyrannical vices are engendered. Cabanis remarks, and the fact is worthy of the greatest attention,—'Presque tous les grands scélérats sont des hommes d'une structure organique vigoureuse, remarquables par la fermeté et la tenacité de leurs fibres musculaires.' It is evident, therefore, how deeply it concerns the happiness of mankind, that the mental trains, which this circumstance has a tendency to raise, should be accurately known, as thus alone the means can be known, how that which is hurtful may be avoided, that which is useful be introduced.

Of beauty and deformity, as circumstances affecting the mental trains, much will not be necessary to be said. Illustrations will occur to every body, to prove, that their power is not inconsiderable; so little, however, has been done to ascertain the facts, and record them in the best possible order, that any thing which deserves the name of knowledge on the subject hardly exists; and the principal service we can render is to point it out for study; to exhort future inquirers to observe diligently the trains which flow from beauty and deformity as their source, and to trace to the largest possible sequences, as above described, the connexions which take place between them. Beauty and deformity, it may be observed, operate upon the mental trains in somewhat a different way from health and disease; rather mediately than immediately. It is the idea of their effect upon other people that is the more immediate cause of the trains to which they give occasion. The idea that beauty commands their favourable regards, is apt to introduce the well known trains, denoted by the terms, vanity, pride, contemptuousness, trains not very favourable to the virtues. The idea that deformity is apt to excite their unfavourable regards, is often observed to lead to acuteness and vigour of intellect, employed as instruments of protection, but to moroseness, and even malignity of temper. The mode, however, in which beauty and deformity operate upon the mental trains, namely, through the idea of their effect upon other people, is common to them with a great many other advantages or disadvantages, which derive their value chiefly from their influence upon other people; and materials for the illustration of this subject have been supplied by various writers upon the human mind.

To the word Temperament, no very precise idea has hitherto been annexed. It may be conceived in the following manner: The bodily structure, the composition of elements in the body of every individual, is different from that in the body of any other. It is observed, however, that the composition is more nearly resembling in some, than in others; that those who thus resemble may be arranged in groups; and that they may all be comprehended in four of five great classes. The circumstances, in which their bodily composition agrees, so as to constitute one of those large classes, have been called the Temperament; and each of those more remarkable characters of the body has been observed to be attended with a peculiar character in the train of ideas. But the illustration of the trains of ideas, and hence of the qualities of mind, which are apt to be introduced by temperament, and by the diversities of age and of sex, we are obliged, by the rapid absorption of the space allotted us wholly to omit. The subject in itself is not very mysterious. Accurate observation, and masterly recordation alone are required. To be sure, the same may be said of every object of human inquiry. But in some cases, it is not so easy to conceive perfectly what observation and recordation mean. On these topics, also, we are happy to say, that Cabanis really affords very considerable helps.

2. We come now to the second sort of physical circumstances, which have the power of introducing habitually certain trains of ideas, and hence of impressing permanent tendencies on the mind,—the circumstances which are external to the body. Some of these are of very great importance. The first is Aliment.

Aliment is good or evil, by quality and quantity. Hartley has remarked long ago, that though all the impressions from which ideas are copied, are made on the extremities of the nerves which are ramified on the surface of the body, and supply the several organs of sense, other impressions are nevertheless made on the extremities of the nerves which are ramified on the internal parts of our bodies, and that many of those impressions are associated with trains of ideas; that the impressions made upon the extremities of the nerves which are ramified on the alimentary canal, are associated with the greatest number of those trains; and of such trains, that some are favourable to happiness, some altogether the reverse. If the quantity and quality of the aliment be the principal cause of those impressions, here is a physiological reason, of the greatest importance, for an accurate observation and recordation of the events occurring in this part of the field; what antecedents are attended by what consequents, and what the largest sequences that can be traced. Cabanis confirmed the doctrine of Hartley with regard to the internal impressions, and added another class. He said that not only the extremities of the nerves which terminate internally, but the centre of the nervous influence, the brain itself, received impressions, and that thus there were no fewer than three sources of mental and corporeal movements of man; one external, from which almost all our distinct ideas are copied; and two internal, which exert a very great influence upon the trains of ideas, and hence upon the actions of which these trains are the antecedents or cause.

On this too, as on most of the other topics, belonging to the physical branch of education, we must note, as still uncollected, the knowledge which is required. It is understood in a general way, that deep impressions are by this means made upon the mind; but how they are made, is a knowledge which, in any such detail and accuracy as to afford useful practical rules, is nearly wanting. There is a passage in Hartley, which we esteem it important to quote: 'The sense of feeling may be distinguished into that of the external surface of the body, and that of the cavities of the nose, mouth, fauces, alimentary duct, pelvis, of the kidneys, uterus, bladder of urine, gall bladder, follicles, and ducts of the glands, &c. The sensibility is much greater in the last than in the first, because the impressions can more easily penetrate through the soft epithelium with which the internal cavities are invested. In the mouth and nose this sensibility is so great, and attended with such distinguishing circumstances, as to have the names of taste and smell assigned respectively to the sensations impressed upon the papillæ of these two organs.' . . . 'The taste may also be distinguished into two kinds; viz. the general one which extends itself to the insides of the lips and cheeks, to the palate, fauces, œsophagus, stomach, and whole alimentary duct, quite down to the anus. . . . The pleasures of the taste, considered as extending itself from the mouth through the whole alimentary duct, are very considerable, and frequently repeated; they must, therefore, be one chief means by which pleasurable states are introduced into the brain and nervous system. These pleasurable states must, after some time, leave miniatures of themselves, sufficiently strong to be called up upon slight occasions, viz. from a variety of associations with the common visible and audible objects, and to illuminate these and their ideas. When groups of these miniatures have been long and closely connected with particular objects, they coalesce into one complex idea, appearing, however, to be a simple one; and so begin to be transferred upon other objects, and even upon tastes back again, and so on without limits. And from this way of reasoning it may now appear, that a great part of our intellectual pleasures are ultimately deducible from those of taste; and that one principal final cause of the greatness and constant recurrency of these pleasures, from our first infancy to the extremity of old age, is to introduce and keep up pleasurable states in the brain, and to connect them with foreign objects. The social pleasures seem, in a particular manner, to be derived from this source, since it has been customary in all ages and nations, and is in a manner necessary, that we should enjoy the pleasures of taste in conjunction with our relations, friends, and neighbours. In like manner, nauseous tastes and painful impressions upon the alimentary duct give rise and strength to mental pains. The most common of these painful impressions is that from excess, and the consequent indigestion. This excites and supports those uneasy states, which attend upon melancholy, fear, and sorrow. It appears also to me, that these states are introduced in a great degree during sleep, during the frightful dreams, agitations, and oppressions, that excess in diet occasions in the night. These dreams and disorders are often forgotten; but the uneasy states of body which then happen, leave vestiges of themselves, which increase in number and strength every day from the continuance of the cause, till at last they are ready to be called up in crowds upon slight occasions, and the unhappy person is unexpectedly, and at once, as it were, seized with a great degree of the hypochondriac distemper, the obvious cause appearing no ways proportionable to the effect. And thus it may appear that there ought to be a great reciprocal influence between the mind and alimentary duct, agreeably to common observation.' Cabanis, in like manner, says, 'Quoique les médecins aient dit plusieurs choses hazardées, touchant l'effet des substances alimentaries sur les organs de la pensée, ou sur les principes physiques de nos penchans, il n'en est pas moins certain que les differentes causes que nous appliquons journellement à nos corps, pour en renouveller les mouvements, agissent avec une grande efficacité sur nos dispositions morales. On se rend plus propre aux travaux de l'esprit par certaines precautions de régime, par l'usage, ou la suppression de certains alimens. Quelques personnes ont été guéries de violens accés de colère, auxquels elles étoient sujêtes, par la seule diète pythagorique, et dans le cas même où des délires furieux troublent toutes les facultés de l'âme, l'emploi journalier de certaines nourritures ou de certaines boissons, l'impression d'une certaine température de l'air, l'aspect de certaines objets; en un mot, un système diététique particulier suffit souvent pour y remener le calme, pour faire tout rentrer dans l'ordre primitif.'

As it is impossible for us here to attempt a full account of the mode in which aliments operate to produce good or bad effects upon the train of ideas, we shall single out that case, which, as operating upon the greatest number of people, is of the greatest importance; we mean that, in which effects are produced by the *poverty* of the diet; proposing, under the term poverty, to include both badness of quality, and defect of quantity. On badness of quality, we shall not spend many words. Aliments are bad in a variety of ways, and to such a degree as to impair the bodily health. Of such, the injurious effect will not be disputed. Others, which have in them no hurtful ingredient, may contain so insignificant a portion of nourishment, that to afford it in the requisite degree, they must produce a hurtful distention of the organs. The saw-dust, which some northern nations use for bread, if depended upon for the whole of their nourishment, would doubtless have this effect. The potato, where solely depended upon, is not, perhaps, altogether free from it. Bad quality, however, is but seldom resorted to, except in consequence of deficient quantity. That is, therefore, the principal point of inquiry.

It is easy to see a great number of ways in which deficient quantity of food operates unfavourably upon the *moral* temper of the mind. As people are ready to sacrifice every thing to the obtaining of a sufficient quantity of food, the want of it implies the most dreadful poverty; that state, in which there is scarcely any source of pleasure, and in which almost every moment is subject to pain. It is found by a very general experience, that a human being, almost constantly in pain, hardly visited by a single pleasure, and almost shut out from hope, loses by degrees all sympathy with his fellow creatures; contracts even a jealousy of their pleasures, and at last a hatred; and would like to see all the rest of mankind as wretched as himself. If he is habitually wretched, and rarely permitted to taste a pleasure, he snatches it with an avidity, and indulges himself with an intemperance, almost unknown to any other man. The evil of insufficient food acts with an influence not less malignant upon the intellectual, than upon the moral part of the human mind. The physiologists account for its influence in this manner. They say, that the signs, by which the living energy is manifested, may be included generally under the term *irritability*, or the power of being put in action by stimulants. It is not necessary for us to be very particular in explaining these terms; a general conception will for the present suffice. A certain degree of this irritability seems necessary to the proper state, or rather the very existence of the animal functions. A succession of stimulants, of a certain degree of frequency and strength, is necessary to preserve that irritability. The most important by far of all the useful stimulants applied to the living organs is food. If this stimulant is applied, in less than a sufficient degree, the irritability is diminished in proportion, and all those manifestations of the living energy which depend upon it, mental as well as corporeal, are impaired; the mind loses a corresponding part of its force. We must refer to the philosophical writers on medicine for illustrations and facts, which we have not room to adduce, but which will not be difficult to collect. Dr Crichton[14] places *poor diet* at the head of a list of causes which 'weaken attention, and consequently debilitate the whole faculties of the mind.'* From this fact, about which there is no dispute, the most important consequences arise. If follows, that when we deliberate about the means of introducing intellectual and moral excellence, into the minds of the principal portion of the people, one of the first things which we are bound to provide for, is, a generous and animating diet. The physical causes must go along with the moral; and nature herself forbids, that you shall make a wise and virtuous people, out of a starving one. Men must be happy themselves, before they can rejoice in the happiness of others; they must have a certain vigour of mind, before they can, in the midst of habitual suffering, resist a presented pleasure; their own lives, and means of well-being, must be worth something, before they can value, so as to respect, the life, or well-being, of any other person. This or that individual may be an extraordinary individual, and exhibit mental excellence in the midst of wretchedness; but a wretched and excellent people never yet has been

* An Inquiry into the Nature and Origin of Mental Derangement, &c. By A. Crichton, M.D.T. 274.

seen on the face of the earth. Though far from fond of paradoxical expressions, we are tempted to say, that a good diet is a necessary part of a good education; for in one very important sense it is emphatically true. In the great body of the people all education is impotent without it.

Labour is the next of the circumstances in our enumeration. We have distinguished labour from action, though action is the genus of which labour is one of the species; because of those species, labour is so much the most important. The muscular operations of the body, by which men generally earn their bread, are the chief part of the particulars which we include under that term. The same distinction is useful here as in the former case; labour is apt to be injurious by its *quality*, and by its *quantity*. That the quality of the labour, in which a man is employed, produces effects, favourable or unfavourable upon his mind, has long been confessed; Dr Smith[15] made the important remark, that the labour in which the great body of the people are employed, has a tendency to grow less and less favourable, as civilization and the arts proceed. The division and subdivision of labour is the principal cause. This confines the attention of the labourer to so small a number of objects, and so narrow a circle of ideas, that the mind receives not that varied exercise, and that portion of aliment, on which almost every degree of mental excellence depends. When the greater part of a man's life is employed in the performance of a few simple operations, in one fixed invariable course, all exercise of ingenuity, all adaptation of means to ends, is wholly excluded, and the faculty lost, as far as disuse can destroy the faculties of the mind. The minds, therefore, of the great body of the people are in danger of really degenerating, while the other elements of civilization are advancing, unless care is taken, by means of the other instruments of education, to counteract those effects which the simplification of the manual processes has a tendency to produce.

The *quantity* of labour is another circumstance which deserves attention in estimating the agents which concur in forming the mind. Labour may be to such a degree severe, as to confine the attention almost wholly to the painful ideas which it brings; and to operate upon the mind with nearly the same effects as an habitual deficiency of food. It operates perhaps still more rapidly; obliterating sympathy, inspiring cruelty and intemperance, rendering impossible the reception of ideas, and paralysing the organs of the mind. The attentive examination, therefore, of the facts of this case, is a matter of first-rate importance. Two things are absolutely certain; that without the bodily labour of the great bulk of mankind the well-being of the species cannot be obtained; and that if the bodily labour of the great bulk of mankind is carried beyond a certain extent, neither intellect, virtue, nor happiness can flourish upon the earth. What, then, is that precious middle point, at which the greatest quantity of good is obtained with the smallest quantity of evil, is, in this part of the subject, the problem to be solved.

The state of defective food and excessive labour, is the state in which we find the great bulk of mankind; the state in which they are either constantly existing, or into which they are every moment threatening to fall. These are two, therefore, in settling the rank among the circumstances which concur in determining the degree of intellect and morality capable of being exhibited in the societies of men, which ought to stand in a very eminent place: the mode of increasing to the utmost, the quantity of intellect, morality, and happiness, in human society, will be very imperfectly understood, till they obtain a new degree of consideration.

We named, besides these, among the physical circumstances which contribute to give permanent characters to the mind, air, temperature, action, and rest. But of these we must leave the illustration wholly to other inquirers. It is mortifying to be obliged to relinquish a subject, on which so much depends, and for which so little has been done, with so very imperfect an attempt for its improvement. We shall, however, have performed a service of some utility to education, if what we have said has any tendency to lead men to a juster estimate of the physical circumstances which concur in fashioning the human mind, and hence to greater industry and care in studying and applying them.

Circumstances of the Moral Kind which operate upon the Mind in the way of Education

The Moral circumstances which determine the mental trains of the human being, and hence the character of his actions, are of so much importance, that to them the term education has been generally confined: or rather, the term education has been generally used in so narrow a sense, that it embraces only one of the four classes into which we have thought it convenient to distribute the moral circumstances which operate to the formation of the human mind.

1. The first of these classes we have comprehended under the term DOMESTIC EDUCATION. To this the groundwork of the character of most individuals is

almost wholly to be traced. The original features are fabricated here; not, indeed, in such a manner as to be unsusceptible of alteration, but in such a manner, decidedly, as to present a good or bad subject for all future means of cultivation. The importance, therefore, of domestic education, needs no additional words to explain it; though it is difficult to restrain a sigh, when we reflect, that it has but now begun to be regarded as within the pale of education; and a few scattered remarks, rather than a full exposition of the subject, is all the information upon it, with which the world has been favoured.

By Domestic Education, we denote all that the child hears and sees, more especially all that it is made to suffer or enjoy at the hands of others, and all that it is allowed or constrained to do, in the house in which it is born and bred, which we shall consider, generally, as the parental.

If we consider, that the mental trains, as explained above, are that upon which every thing depends, and that the mental trains depend essentially upon those sequences among our sensations which have been so frequently experienced as to create a habit of passing from the idea of the one to that of the other, we shall perceive immediately the reasons of what we have advanced.

It seems to be a law of human nature, that the first sensations experienced produced the greatest effects; more especially, that the earliest repetitions of one sensation after another produce the deepest habit; the strongest propensity to pass immediately from the idea of the one to the idea of the other. Common language confirms this law, when it speaks of the susceptibility of the tender mind. On this depends the power of those associations which form some of the most interesting phenomena of human life. From what other cause does it arise, that the hearing of a musical air, which, after a life of absence, recalls the parental mansion, produces as it were a revolution in the whole being? That the sympathies between brothers and sisters are what they are? On what other cause originally is the love of country founded?—that passionate attachment to the soil, the people, the manners, the woods, the rivers, the hills, with which our infant eyes were familiar, which fed our youthful imaginations, and with the presence of which the pleasures of our early years were habitually conjoined!

It is, then, a fact, that the early sequences to which we are accustomed form the primary habits; and that the primary habits are the fundamental character of the man. The consequence is most important; for it follows, that, as soon as the infant, or rather the embryo, begins to feel, the character begins to be formed; and that the habits, which are then contracted, are the most pervading and operative of all. Education, then, or the care of forming the habits, ought to commence, as much as possible, with the period of sensation itself; and, at no period, is its utmost vigilance of greater importance, than the first.

Very unconnected, or very general instructions, are all that can be given upon this subject, till the proper decompositions and recompositions are performed; in other words, till the subject is first analysed, and then systemized; or, in one word, *philosophized*, if we may use that verb in a passive signification. We can, therefore, do little more than exhort to the prosecution of the inquiry.

The steady conception of the End must guide us to

the Means. Happiness is the end; and we have circumscribed the inquiry, by naming Intelligence, Temperance, and Benevolence, of which last the two parts are Generosity and Justice, as the grand qualities of mind, through which this end is to be attained. The question, then, is, how can those early sequences be made to take place on which the habits, conducive to intelligence, temperance, and benevolence, are founded; and how can those sequences, on which are founded the vices opposite to those virtues, be prevented?

Clearness is attained, by disentangling complexity; we ought, therefore, to trace the sequences conducive to each of those qualities in their turn. A part, however, must suffice when we cannot accomplish the whole. Intelligent trains of ideas constitute intelligence. Trains of ideas are intelligent, when the sequences in the ideas correspond to the sequences in nature. A man, for example, knows the order of certain words, when his idea of the one follows that of the other, in the same order in which the events themselves took place. A man is sagacious in devising means for the production of events when his ideas run easily in trains which are at once agreeable to knowledge, that is, to the trains of events, and at the same time new in the combination. They must be agreeable to knowledge; that is, one of the ideas must follow another in the order in which the objects of which they are the ideas follow one another in nature, otherwise the train would consist of mere chimeras, and, having no connexion with things, would be utterly useless. As the event, however, is not in the ordinary course; otherwise sagacity would not be required to give it existence; the ordinary train of antecedents will not suffice; it must be a peculiar train, at once correspondent with nature, and adapted to the end. The earliest trains, produced in the minds of children, should be made to partake as much as possible of those characters. The impressions made upon them should correspond to the great and commanding sequences established among the events on which human happiness principally depends. More explicitly, children ought to be made to see, and hear, and feel, and taste, in the order of the most invariable and comprehensive sequences, in order that the ideas which correspond to their impressions, and follow the same order of succession, may be an exact transcript of nature, and always lead to just anticipations of events. Especially, the pains and pleasures of the infant, the deepest impressions which he receives, ought, from the first moment of sensation, to be made as much as possible to correspond to the real order of nature. The moral procedure of parents is directly the reverse; they strive to defeat the order of nature, in accumulating pleasure for their children, and preventing the arrival of pains, when the children's own conduct would have had very different effects.

Not only are the impressions, from which ideas are copied, made, by the injudicious conduct of those to whom the destiny of infants is confided, to follow an order very different from the natural one, or that in which the grand sequences among events would naturally produce them; but wrong trains of ideas, trains which have no correspondence with the order of events, are often introduced immediately by words, or other signs of the ideas of other men. As we can only give very partial examples of a general error, we may content ourselves with one of the most common. When those who are about children express by their words, or indicate by other signs, that terrific trains of ideas are passing in their minds, when they go into the dark; terrific trains, which have nothing to do with the order of events, come up also in the minds of the children in the dark, and often exercise over them an uncontrollable sway during the whole of their lives.—This is the grand source of wrong education; to this may be traced the greater proportion of all the evil biases of the human mind.—If an order of ideas, corresponding with the order of events, were taught to come up in the minds of children when they go into the dark, they would think of nothing but the real dangers which are apt to attend it, and the precautions which are proper to be taken; they would have no wrong feelings, and their conduct would be nothing but that which prudence, or a right conception of the events, would prescribe.—If the expressions, and other signs of the ideas of those who are about children, indicate that trains, accompanied with desire and admiration, pass in their minds when the rich and powerful are named, trains accompanied with aversion and contempt when the weak and the poor, the foundation is laid of a character stained with servility to those above, and tyranny to those below them. If indication is given to children that ideas of disgust, of hatred, and detestation, are passing in the minds of those about them, when particular descriptions of men are thought of; as men of different religions, different countries, or different political parties in the same country; a similar train becomes habitual in the minds of the children; and those antipathies are generated which infuse so much of its bitterness into the cup of human life.

We can afford to say but very few words on the powers of domestic education with regard to Temperance. That virtue bears a reference to pain and pleasure. The grand object evidently is, to connect with each pain and pleasure those trains of ideas which, according to the order established among events, tend most effectually to increase the sum of pleasures upon the whole, and diminish that of pains. If the early trains create a habit of over-valuing any pleasure or pain, too much will be sacrificed, during life, to obtain the one, or avoid the other, and the sum of happiness, upon the whole, will be impaired. The order in which children receive their impressions, as well as the order of the trains which they copy from others, has a tendency to create impatience under privation; in other words, to make them in prodigious haste to realize a pleasure as soon as desired, to extinguish a pain as soon as felt. A pleasure, however, can be realized in the best possible manner, or a pain removed, only by certain steps,—frequently numerous ones; and if impatience hurries a man to overlook those steps, he may sacrifice more than he gains. The desirable thing would be, that his ideas should always run over those very steps, and none but them; and the skilful use of the powers we have over the impressions and trains of his infancy would lay the strongest foundation for the future happiness of himself, and of all those over whom his actions have any sway. It is by the use of this power that almost every thing is done to create what is called the temper of the individual; to render him irascible on the one hand, or forbearing on the other; severe and unforgiving, or indulgent and placable.

Intelligence and Temperance are sometimes spoken of, as virtues which have a reference to the happiness of the individual himself: Benevolence as a virtue which has a reference to the happiness of others. The truth is, that intelligence and temperance have a reference not less direct to the happiness of others than to that of the possessor; and Benevolence cannot be considered as less essential to his happiness than intelligence and temperance. In reality, as the happiness of the individual is bound up with that of his species, that which affects the happiness of the one, must also, in general, affect that of the other.

It is not difficult, from the expositions we have already given, to conceive in a general way how sequences may take place in the mind of the infant which are favourable to benevolence, and how sequences may take place which are unfavourable to it. The difficulty is, so to bring forward and exhibit the details, as to afford the best possible instruction for practice. We have several books now in our own language, in particular those of Miss Edgeworth,[16] which afford many finely selected instances, and many detached observations of the greatest value, for the cultivation of benevolence in the infant mind. But the great task of the philosopher, that of *theorizing* the whole, is yet to be performed. What we mean by 'theorizing the whole', after the explanations we have already afforded, is not, we should hope, obscure. It is, to observe exactly the facts; to make a perfect collection of them, nothing omitted that is of any importance, nothing included of none; and to record them in that order and form, in which all that is best to be done in practice can be most immediately and certainly perceived.

The order of the impressions which are made upon the child, by the spontaneous order of events, is, to a certain degree, favourable to benevolence. The pleasures of those who are about him are most commonly the cause of pleasure to himself; their pains of pain. When highly pleased, they are commonly more disposed to exert themselves to gratify him. A period of pain or grief in those about him, is a period of gloom—a period in which little is done for pleasure—a period in which the pleasures of the child are apt to be overlooked. Trains of pleasurable ideas are thus apt to arise in his mind, at the thought of the pleasurable condition of those around him; trains of painful ideas at the thought of the reverse; and he is thus led to have an habitual desire for the one, aversion to the other. But if pleasures, whencesoever derived, of those about him, are apt to be the cause of good to himself, those pleasures which they derive from himself, are in a greater degree the cause of good to himself. If those about him are disposed to exert themselves to please him when they are pleased themselves, they are disposed to exert themselves in a much greater degree to please him, in particular, when it is he who is the cause of the pleasure they enjoy. A train of ideas, in the highest degree pleasurable, may thus habitually pass through his mind at the thought of happiness to others produced by himself; a train of ideas, in the highest degree painful, at the thought of misery to others produced by himself. In this manner the foundation of a life of beneficence is laid.

The business of a skilful education is, so to arrange the circumstances by which the child is surrounded, that the impressions made upon him shall be in the order most conducive to this happy result. The impressions, too, which are made originally upon the child, are but one of the causes of the trains which are rendered habitual to him, and which, therefore, obtain a leading influence in his mind. When he is often made to conceive the trains of other men, by the words, or other signs by which their feelings are betokened, those borrowed trains become also habitual, and exert a similar influence on the mind. This, then, is another of the instruments of education. When the trains, signified to the child, of the ideas in the minds of those about him are trains of pleasure at the thought of the happiness of other human beings, trains of the opposite kind at the conception of their misery; and when such trains are still more pleasurable or painful as the happiness or misery is produced by themselves, the association becomes in time sufficiently powerful to govern the life.

The grand object of human desire is a command over the wills of other men. This may be attained, either by qualities and acts which excite their love and admiration, or by those which excite their terror. When the education is so wisely conducted as to make the train run habitually from the conception of the good end to the conception of the good means; and as often, too, as the good means are conceived, viz. the useful and beneficial qualities, to make the train run on to the conception of the great reward, the command over the wills of men; an association is formed which impels the man through life to pursue the great object of desire, fitting himself to be, and by actually becoming, the instrument of the greatest possible benefit to his fellow men.

But, unhappily, a command over the wills of men may be obtained by other means than by doing them good; and these, when a man can command them, are the shortest, the easiest, and the most effectual. These other means are all summed up in a command over the pains of other men. When a command over the wills of other men is pursued by the instrumentality of pain, it leads to all the several degrees of vexation, injustice, cruelty, oppression, and tyranny. It is, in truth, the grand source of all wickedness, of all the evil which man brings upon man. When the education is so deplorably bad as to allow an association to be formed in the mind of the child between the grand object of desire, the command over the wills of other men, and the fears and pains of other men, as the means; the foundation is laid of the bad character,—the bad son, the bad brother, the bad husband, the bad father, the bad neighbour, the bad magistrate, the bad citizen,—to sum up all in one word, the bad man. Yet, true, it is, a great part of education is still so conducted as to form that association. The child, while it yet hangs at the breast, is often allowed to find out by experience, that crying, and the annoyance which it gives, is that by which chiefly it can command the services of its nurse, and obtain the pleasures which it desires. There is not one child in fifty, who has not learned to make its cries and wailings an instrument of power; very often they are an instrument of absolute tyranny. When the evil grows to excess, the vulgar say the child is spoiled. Not only is the child allowed to exert an influence over the wills of others, by means of their pains; it finds, that frequently, sometimes most frequently, its own will is needlessly and unduly commanded by the same means, pain, and the fear of pain. All these sensations concur in establishing a firm association between the idea of the grand object of desire, command over the acts of other men, and the idea of pain and terror, as the means of acquiring it. That those who have been subject to tyranny, are almost always desirous of being tyrants in their turn; that is to say, that a strong association has been formed in their minds, between the ideas of pleasure and dignity, on the one hand, and those of the exercise of tyranny, on the other, is a matter of old and invariable observation. An anecdote has just been mentioned to us, so much in point, that we will repeat it, as resting on its own probability, though it is hearsay evidence (very good, however, of its kind) on which we have received it. At Eton, in consequence, it is probable, of the criticisms which the press has usefully made upon the system of *fagging* (as it is called), at the public schools, a proposition was lately made, among the boys themselves, for abolishing it. The idea originated with the elder boys, who were in possession of the power; a power of a very unlimited and formidable description; and by them was warmly supported. It was, however, opposed with still greater vehemence by the junior boys, the boys who were then the victims of it. The expected pleasure of tyrannizing in their turn, outweighed the pain of their present slavery. In this case, too, as in most others, the sources of those trains which govern us are two—the impressions made upon ourselves, and the trains which we copy from others. Besides the impressions just recounted, if the trains which pass in the minds of those by whom the child is surrounded, and which he is made to conceive by means of their words, and other signs, lead constantly from the idea of command over the wills of other men, as the grand object of desire, to the ideas of pain and terror as the means, the repetition of the copied trains increases the effect of the native impressions, and establishes and confirms the maleficent character. These are the few things we can afford to adduce upon the subject of Domestic Education.

2. In the next place comes that which we have denominated Technical Education. To this the

term Education has been commonly confined; or, rather, the word Education has been used in a sense so unhappily restricted, that it has extended only to a part of that which we call Technical Education. It has not extended to all the arts, but only to those which have been denominated liberal.

The question here occurs—What is the sort of education required for the different classes of society, and what should be the difference in the training provided for each? Before we can treat explicitly of technical education, we must endeavour to show, in what manner, at least, this question ought to be resolved.

There are certain qualities, the possession of which is desirable in all classes. There are certain qualities, the possession of which is desirable in some, not in others. As far as those qualities extend which ought to be common to all, there ought to be a correspondent training for all. It is only in respect to those qualities which are not desirable in all, that a difference in the mode of training is required.

What then are the qualities, the possession of which is desirable in all? They are the qualities which we have already named as chiefly subservient to the happiness of the individual himself, and of other men; Intelligence, Temperance, and Benevolence. It is very evident that these qualities are desirable in all men; and if it were possible to get them all in the highest possible degree in all men, so much the more would human nature be exalted.

The chief difficulty respects Intelligence; for it will be readily allowed, that almost equal care ought to be taken, in all classes, of the trains leading to the settled dispositions which the terms Temperance and Benevolence denote. Benevolence, as we have above described it, can hardly be said to be of more importance to the happiness of man in one class than in another. If we bear in mind, also, the radical meaning of Temperance, that it is the steady habit of resisting a present desire, for the sake of a greater good, we shall readily grant, that it is not less necessary to happiness in one rank of life than in another. It is only necessary to see, that temperance, though always the same disposition, is not always exerted on the same objects, in the different conditions of life. It is no demand of temperance, in the man who can afford it, to deny himself animal food; it may be an act of temperance in the man whose harder circumstances require that he should limit himself to coarser fare. It is also true, that the trains which lead to Temperance and Benevolence may be equally cultivated in all classes. The impressions which persons are made to receive, and the trains of others which they are made to copy, may, with equal certainty, be guided to the generating of those two qualities in all the different classes of society. We deem it unnecessary, (here indeed, it is impossible) to enter into the details of what may be done in the course of technical education, to generate, or to confirm, the dispositions of Temperance and Benevolence. It can be nothing more than the application of the principles which we developed, when we endeavoured to show in what manner the circumstances of domestic education might be employed for generating the trains on which these mental qualities depend.

Technical Education, we shall then consider, as having chiefly to do with *Intelligence*.

The first question, as we have said before, respects what is desirable for all,—the second, what is desirable for each of the several classes. Till recently, it was denied, that intelligence was a desirable quality in the great body of the people; and as intelligence is power, such is an unavoidable opinion in the breasts of those who think that the human race ought to consist of two classes,—one that of the oppressors, another that of the oppressed. The concern which is now felt for the education of the working classes, shows that we have made a great step in knowledge, and in that genuine morality which ever attends it.

The analysis of the ideas decides the whole matter at once. If education be to communicate the art of happiness; and if intelligence consists of two parts, a knowledge of the order of those events of nature on which our pleasures and pains depend, and the sagacity which discovers the best means for the attaining of ends; the question, whether the people should be educated, is the same with the question, whether they should be happy or miserable. The question, whether they should have more or less of intelligence, is merely the question, whether they should have more or less of misery, when happiness might be given in its stead. It has been urged that men are, by daily experience, evinced not to be happy, not to be moral, in proportion to their knowledge. It is a shallow objection. Long ago it was observed by Hume, that knowledge and its accompaniments, morality and happiness, may not be strictly conjoined in every individual, but that they are infallibly so in every age, and in every country. The reason is plain; a natural cause may be hindered of its operation in one particular instance, though in a great variety of instances it is sure to prevail. Besides, there may be a good deal of knowledge in an individual, but not knowledge of the best things; this cannot easily happen in a whole people; neither the whole nor the greater part will miss the right objects of knowledge, when knowledge is generally diffused.

As evidence of the vast progress which we have made in right thinking upon this subject, we cannot help remarking, that even Milton and Locke, though both men of great benevolence toward the larger family of mankind, and both men whose sentiments were democratical, yet seem, in their writings on education, to have had in view no education but that of the *gentleman*. It had not presented itself, even to their minds, that education was a blessing in which the indigent orders could be made to partake.

As we strive for an equal degree of justice, an equal degree of temperance, an equal degree of veracity, in the poor as in the rich, so ought we to strive for an equal degree of intelligence, if there were not a preventing cause. It is absolutely necessary for the existence of the human race, that labour should be performed, that food should be produced, and other things provided, which human welfare requires. A large proportion of mankind is required for this labour. Now, then, in regard to all this portion of mankind, that labours, only such a portion of time can by them be given to the acquisition of intelligence, as can be abstracted from labour. The difference between intelligence and the other qualities desirable in the mind of man, is this, That much of time, exclusively devoted to the fixing of the associations on which the other qualities depend is not necessary; such trains may go on while other things are attended to, and amid the whole of the business of life. The case is to a certain extent, the same with intelligence; but, to a great extent, it is not. Time must be exclusively devoted to the acquisition of it; and there are degrees of command over knowledge to which the whole period of human life is not more than sufficient. There are degrees, therefore, of intelligence, which must be reserved to those who are not obliged to labour.

The question is (and it is a question which none can exceed in importance), What is the degree attainable by the most numerous class? To this we have no doubt, it will, in time, very clearly appear, that a most consolatory answer may be given. We have no doubt it will appear that a very high degree is attainable by them. It is now almost universally acknowledged, that, on all conceivable accounts, it is desirable that the great body of the people should not be wretchedly poor; that when the people are wretchedly poor, all classes are vicious, all are hateful, and all are unhappy. If so far raised above wretched poverty, as to be capable of being virtuous; though it be still necessary for them to earn their bread by the sweat of their brow, they are not bound down to such incessant toil as to have no time for the acquisition of knowledge, and the exercise of intellect. Above all, a certain portion of the first years of life are admirably available to this great end. With a view to the productive powers of their very labour, it is desirable that the animal frame should not be devoted to it before a certain age, before it has approached the point of maturity. This holds in regard to the lower animals; a horse is less valuable, less, in regard to that very labour for which he is valuable at all, if he is forced upon it too soon. There is an actual loss, therefore, even in productive powers, even in good economy, and in the way of health and strength, if the young of the human species are bound close to labour before they are fifteen or sixteen years of age. But if those years are skilfully employed in the acquisition of knowledge, in rendering all those trains habitual on which intelligence depends, it may be easily shown that a very high degree of intellectual acquirements may be gained; that a firm foundation may be laid for a life of mental action, a life of wisdom, and reflection, and ingenuity, even in those by whom the most ordinary labour will fall to be performed. In proof of this, we may state, that certain individuals in London, a few years ago, some of them men of great consideration among their countrymen, devised a plan for filling up those years with useful instruction; a plan which left the elements of hardly any branch of knowledge unprovided for; and at an expense which would exceed the means of no class of a population, raised as much above wretched poverty as all men profess to regard as desirable. Mr Bentham called this plan of instruction by the Greek name *Chrestomathia*;[17] and developed his own ideas of the objects and mode of instruction, with that depth and comprehension which belong to him, in a work which he published under that name.* Of the practicability of the scheme no competent judge has ever doubted; and the difficulty of collecting funds is the only reason why it has not been demonstrated by experiment, how much of that intelligence which is desirable for all may be communicated to all.†

* *Chrestomathia*, being a collection of papers, explanatory of the design of an institution proposed to be set on foot, under the name of Chrestomathic day school, &c. By Jeremy Bentham, Esq.

† We mention with extraordinary satisfaction, that an idea of education, hardly less extensive than what is here alluded to, has been adopted by that enlightened and indefatigable class of men, the Baptist Missionaries in India, for the population, poor as well as ignorant, of those extensive and populous regions. A small volume, entitled '*Hints relative to Native Schools, together with the Outline of an Institution for their Extension and Management*,' was printed at the mission press at Serampore in 1816; and, as it cannot come into the hands of many of our readers, we gladly copy from it the following passage, in hopes that the example may be persuasive with many of our countrymen at home.

'It is true, that when these helps are provided, namely, a correct system of orthography, a sketch of grammar, a simplified system of arithmetic, and an extended vocabulary, little is done beyond laying the foundation. Still, however, this foundation must be laid, if any superstructure of knowledge and virtue be attempted relative to the inhabitants of India. Yet, were the plan to stop here, something would have been done. A peasant or an artificer, thus rendered capable of writing as well as reading his own language with propriety, and made acquainted with the principles of arithmetic, would be less liable to become a prey to fraud among his own countrymen; and far better able to claim for himself that protection from oppression which it is the desire of every enlightened government to grant. But the chief advantage derivable from this plan is, its facilitating the reception of ideas which may enlarge and bless the mind in a high degree,—ideas for which India must be indebted to the West, at present the seat of science, and for the communication of which, generations yet unborn, will pour benedictions on the British name.

'1. To this, then, might be added a concise, but perspicuous account of the solar system, preceded by so much of the laws of motion, of attraction, and gravity, as might be necessary to render the solar system plain and intelligible. These ideas, however, should not be communicated in the form of a treatise, but in that of simple axioms, delivered in short and perspicuous sentences. This method comes recommended by several considerations;—it agrees with the mode in which doctrines are communicated in the *Hindoo Shastras*, and is therefore congenial with the ideas of even the learned among them; it would admit of these sentences being written from dictation, and even committed to memory with advantage, as well as of their being easily retained; and, finally, the conciseness of this method would allow of a multitude of truths and facts relative to astronomy, geography, and the principal phenomena of nature, being brought before youth within a very small compass.

'2. This abstract of the solar system might be followed by a compendious view of geography on the same plan—that of comprising every particular in concise but luminous sentences. In this part it would be proper to describe Europe particularly, because of its importance in the present state of the world; and Britain might, with propriety, be allowed to occupy in the compendium, that preeminence among the nations which the God of Providence has given her.

'3. To these might be added a number of popular truths and facts relative to natural philosophy. In the present improved state of knowledge, a thousand things have been ascertained relative to light, heat, air, water to meteorology, mineralogy, chemistry, and natural history, of which the ancients had but a partial knowledge, and of which the natives of the East have as yet scarcely the faintest idea. These facts, now so clearly ascertained, could be conveyed in a very short compass of language, although the process of reasoning, which enables the mind to account for them, occupies many volumes. A knowledge of the facts themselves, however, would be almost invaluable to the Hindoos, as these facts would rectify and enlarge their ideas of the various objects of nature around them; and while they, in general, delighted as well as informed those who read them, they might inflame a few minds of a superior order with an unquenchable desire to know *why* these things are so, and thus urge them to those studies, which in Europe have led to the discovery of these important facts.

'4. To this view of the solar system of the earth, and the various objects it contains, might, with great advantage, be added such a compendium of history and chronology united, as should bring them acquainted with the state of the world in past ages, and with the principal events which have occurred since the creation of the world. With the creation it should commence, describe the primitive state of man, the entrance of evil, the corruption of the antediluvian age, the flood, and the peopling of the earth anew from one family, in which the compiler should avail himself of all the light thrown on this subject by modern research and investigation; he should particularly notice the nations of the east, incorporating, in their proper place, the best accounts we now have both of India and China. He should go on to notice the call of Abraham, the giving of the decalogue, the gradual revelations of the Scriptures of Truth, the settlement of Greece, its mythology, the Trojan war, the four great monarchies, the advent of the Saviour of men, the persecutions of the Christian church, the rise of Mahometanism, the origin of the papacy, the invention of printing, of gunpowder, and the mariner's compass, the reformation, the discovery of the passage to India by sea, and the various discoveries of modern science. Such a synopsis of history and chronology, composed on the same plan, that of comprising each event in a concise but perspicuous sentence, would exceedingly enlarge their ideas relative to the state of the world, certainly not to the disadvantage of Britain, whom God has now so exalted as to render her almost the arbitress of nations.

'5. Lastly, It would be highly proper to impart to them just ideas of themselves, relative both to body and mind, and to a future state of existence, by what may be termed a Compendium of Ethics and Morality. The complete absence of all just ideas of this kind, is the chief cause of that degradation of public morals so evident in this country.

Beside the knowledge or faculties, which all classes should possess in common, there are branches of knowledge and art, which they cannot all acquire, and, in respect to which, education must undergo a corresponding variety. The apprenticeships, for example, which youths are accustomed to serve to the useful arts, we regard as a branch of their education. Whether these apprenticeships, as they have hitherto been managed, have been good instruments of education, is a question of importance, about which there is now, among enlightened men, hardly any diversity of opinion. When the legislature undertakes to do for every man, what every man has abundant motives to do for himself, and better means than the legislature; the legislature takes a very unnecessary, commonly a not very innocent trouble. Into the details, however, of the best mode of teaching, to the working people, the arts by which the different commodities useful or agreeable to man are provided, we cannot possibly enter. We must content ourselves with marking it out as a distinct branch of the subject, and an important object of study.

With respect to the education of that class of society who have wealth and time for the acquisition of the highest measure of intelligence, there is one question to

'These various compendiums, after being written from dictation, in the manner described in the next section, might also furnish matter for reading; and when it is considered that, in addition to the sketch of grammar, the vocabulary, and the system of arithmetic, they include a view of the solar system, a synopsis of geography, a collection of facts relative to natural objects, an abstract of general history, and a compendium of ethics and morality, they will be found to furnish sufficient matter for reading while youth are at school.'

Why should not the same idea be pursued in England, and as much knowledge conveyed to the youth of all classes at school, as the knowledge of the age, and the allotted period of schooling will admit?

which every body must be prepared with an answer. If it be asked, whether, in the constitution of any establishment for the education of this class; call it university, call it college, school, or any thing else; there ought to be a provision for perpetual improvement; a provision to make the institution keep pace with the human mind; or whether, on the other hand, it ought to be so constituted as that there should not only be no provision for, but a strong spirit of resistance to, all improvement, a passion of adherence to whatever was established in a dark age, and a principle of hatred to those by whom improvement should be proposed; all indifferent men will pronounce, that such institution would be a curse rather than a blessing. That he is a *progressive* being, is the grand distinction of Man. He is the only progressive being upon this globe. When he is the most rapidly progressive, then he most completely fulfils his destiny. An institution for *education* which is hostile to progression, is, therefore, the most preposterous, and vicious thing, which the mind of man can conceive.

There are several causes which tend to impair the utility of old and opulent establishments for education. Their love of ease makes them love easy things, if they can derive from them as much credit, as they would from others which are more difficult. They endeavour, therefore, to give an artificial value to trifles. Old practices, which have become a hackneyed routine, are commonly easier than improvements; accordingly, they oppose improvements, even when it happens that they have no other interest in the preservation of abuses. Hardly is there a part of Europe in which the universities are not recorded in the annals of education, as the enemies of all innovation. 'A peine la compagnie de Jesus,' says d'Alembert,[18] 'commençait elle à se montrer en France, qu'elle essuya des difficultés sans nombre pour s'y établir. Les universités surtout firent les plus grands efforts, pour écarter ces nouveaux venus. Les Jesuites s'annonçaient pour enseigner gratuitement, ils comptoient déjà parmi eux des hommes savans et célèbres, supérieures peut être à ceux dont les universités pouvaient se glorifier; l'interêt et la vanité pouvaient donc suffire à leurs adversaires pour chercher à les exclure. On se rappelle les contradictions semblables que les ordres mendians essuyerent de ces mêmes universités quand ils voulurent s'y introduire; contradictions fondées à peu près sur les mêmes motifs.' (*Destruction des Jesuites en France.*) The celebrated German philosopher, Wolf,[19] remarks the aversion of the universities to all improvement, as a notorious fact, derived from adequate motives: 'Non adeo impune turbare licet scholarium quietem, et docentibus lucrosam, et discentibus jucundam.'—(Wolfii *Logica*, Dedic. p. 2.)

But though such and so great are the evil tendencies which are to be guarded against in associated seminaries of education; evil tendencies which are apt to be indefinitely increased, when they are united with an ecclesiastical establishment, because, whatever the vices of the ecclesiastical system, the universities have in that case an interest to bend the whole of their force to the support of those vices, and to that end to vitiate the human mind, which can only be rendered the friend of abuses in proportion as it is vitiated intellectually, or morally, or both; it must, notwithstanding, be confessed, that there are great advantages in putting it in the power of the youth to obtain all the branches of their education in one place; even in assembling a certain number of them together, when the principle of emulation acts with powerful effect; and in carrying on the complicated process according to a regular plan, under a certain degree of discipline, and with the powerful spur of publicity. All this ought not to be rashly sacrificed; nor does there appear to be any insuperable difficulty, in devising a plan for the attainment of all those advantages, without the evils which have more or less adhered to all the collegiate establishments which Europe has yet enjoyed.

After the consideration of these questions, we ought next to describe, and prove by analysis, the exercises which would be most conducive in forming those virtues which we include under the name of intelligence. But it is very evident, that this is a matter of detail far too extensive for so limited a design as ours. And though, in common language, Education means hardly any thing more than making the youth perform those exercises; and a treatise on Education means little more than an account of them; we must content ourselves with marking the place which the inquiry would occupy in a complete system, and proceed to offer a few remarks on the two remaining branches of the subject, *Social Education*, and *Political Education*.

The branches of moral education, heretofore spoken of, operate upon the individual in the first period of life, and when he is not as yet his own master. The two just now mentioned operate upon the whole period of life, but more directly and powerfully after the technical education is at an end, and the youth is launched into the world under his own control.

3. SOCIAL EDUCATION is that in which Society is the Institutor. That the Society in which an individual moves produces great effects upon his mode of thinking and acting, every body knows by indubitable ex-

perience. The object is, to ascertain the extent of this influence, the mode in which it is brought about, and hence the means of making it operate in a good, rather than an evil direction.

The force of this influence springs from two sources: the principle of imitation; and the power of the society over our happiness and misery.

We have already shown, that when, by means of words and other signs of what is passing in the minds of other men, we are made to conceive, step by step, the trains which are governing them, those trains, by repetition, become habitual to our own minds, and exert the same influence over us as those which arise from our own impressions. It is very evident, that those trains which are most habitually passing in the minds of all those individuals by whom we are surrounded, must be made to pass with extraordinary frequency through our own minds, and must, unless where extraordinary means are used to prevent them from producing their natural effect, engross to a proportional degree the dominion of our minds. With this slight indication of this source of the power which society usurps over our minds, that is, of the share which it has in our education, we must content ourselves, and pass to the next.

Nothing is more remarkable in human nature, than the intense desire which we feel of the favourable regards of mankind. Few men could bear to live under an exclusion from the breast of every human being. It is astonishing how great a portion of all the actions of men are directed to these favourable regards, and to no other object. The greatest princes, the most despotical masters of human destiny, when asked what they aim at by their wars and conquests, would answer, if sincere, as Frederic of Prussia answered, *pour faire parler de soi*;

to occupy a large space in the admiration of mankind. What are the ordinary pursuits of wealth and of power, which kindle to such a height the ardour of mankind? Not the mere love of eating and of drinking, or all the physical objects together, which wealth can purchase or power command. With these every man is in the long run speedily satisfied. It is the easy command, which those advantages procure over the favourable regards of society,—it is this which renders the desire of wealth unbounded, and gives it that irresistible influence which it possesses in directing the human mind.

Whatever, then, are the trains of thought, whatever is the course of action which most strongly recommends us to the favourable regards of those among whom we live, these we feel the strongest motive to cultivate and display; whatever trains of thought and course of action expose us to their unfavourable regards, these we feel the strongest motives to avoid. These inducements, operating upon us continually, have an irresistible influence in creating habits, and in moulding, that is, educating us, into a character conformable to the society in which we move. This is the general principle; it might be illustrated in detail by many of the most interesting and instructive phenomena of human life; it is an illustration, however, which we cannot pursue.

To what extent the habits and character, which those influences tend to produce, may engross the man, will no doubt depend, to a certain degree, upon the powers of the domestic and technical education which he has undergone. We may conceive that certain trains might, by the skilful employment of the early years, be rendered so habitual as to be uncontrollable by any habits which the subsequent period of life could induce, and that those trains might be the decisive ones, on which intelligent and moral conduct depends. The influence of a vicious and ignorant society would in this case be greatly reduced; but still, the actual rewards and punishments which society has to bestow, upon those who please, and those who displease it; the good and evil, which it gives, or withholds, are so great, that to adopt the opinions which it approves, to perform the acts which it admires, to acquire the character, in short, which it 'delighteth to honour,' can seldom fail to be the leading object of those of whom it is composed. And as this potent influence operates upon those who conduct both the domestic education and the technical, it is next to impossible that the trains which are generated, even during the time of their operation, should not fall in with, instead of counteracting, the trains which the social education produces; it is next to impossible, therefore, that the whole man should not take the shape which that influence is calculated to impress upon him.

4. The POLITICAL EDUCATION is the last, which we have undertaken to notice, of the agents employed in forming the character of man. The importance of this subject has not escaped observation. Some writers have treated of it in a comprehensive and systematical manner. And a still greater number have illustrated it by occasional and striking remarks. It is, nevertheless, true, that the full and perfect exposition of it yet remains to be made.

The Political Education is like the key-stone of the arch; the strength of the whole depends upon it. We have seen that the strength of the Domestic and the Technical Education depends almost entirely upon the

Social. Now it is certain, that the nature of the Social depends almost entirely upon the Political; and the most important part of the Physical (that which operates with greatest force upon the greatest number, the state of aliment and labour of the lower classes), is, in the long-run, determined by the action of the political machine. The play, therefore, of the political machine acts immediately upon the mind, and with extraordinary power; but this is not all; it also acts upon almost every thing else by which the character of the mind is apt to be formed.

It is a common observation, that such as is the direction given to the desires and passions of men, such is the character of the men. The direction is given to the desires and passions of men by one thing, and one alone; the means by which the grand objects of desire may be attained. Now this is certain, that the means by which the grand objects of desire may be attained, depend almost wholly upon the political machine. When the political machine is such, that the grand objects of desire are seen to be the natural prizes of great and virtuous conduct—of high services to mankind, and of the generous and amiable sentiments from which great endeavours in the service of mankind naturally proceed—it is natural to see diffused among mankind a generous ardour in the acquisition of all those admirable qualities which prepare a man for admirable actions; great intelligence, perfect self-command, and over-ruling benevolence. When the political machine is such that the grand objects of desire are seen to be the reward, not of virtue, not of talent, but of subservience to the will, and command over the affections of the ruling few; interest with the *man above* to be the only sure means to the next step in wealth, or power, or consideration, and so on; the means of pleasing the man above become, in that case, the great object of pursuit. And as the favours of the man above are necessarily limited—as some, therefore, of the candidates for his favour can only obtain the objects of their desire by disappointing others—the arts of supplanting rise into importance; and the whole of that tribe of faculties denoted by the words intrigue, flattery, back-biting, treachery, &c., are the fruitful offspring of that political education which government, where the interests of the subject many are but a secondary object, cannot fail to produce.

SCHOOLS FOR ALL, IN PREFERENCE TO SCHOOLS FOR CHURCHMEN ONLY

The nation is aware that the cry of 'The Church is in danger!' has been raised, upon the occasion of a new and promising attempt to educate the children of the poor.

There are certain general things of which mankind have acquired a general experience. This experience affords, with regard to those things, pre-existing evidence for each occurring instance, if not infallible, at any rate highly presumptive.

The cry of 'The Church is in danger!' is one of the things of which the world has acquired a general experience. Now let ecclesiastical history be ransacked; let it be explored with the utmost minuteness from the beginning to the end; hardly in any instance will the cry of 'The Church is in danger!' be found to have been raised except for the purpose of doing mischief to mankind. Many are the instances in which it has been raised for the purpose of producing trains of the most atrocious actions. In still more numerous instances, particularly in our own country, it has been raised to prevent the introduction of some benefit to mankind. Two of the greatest blessings, competent to human nature, in its social capacity, are *liberty* and *knowledge*. Against these, the cry of 'The Church is in danger!' has hardly ever failed to be set up. So long as ignorance was prevailing; so long as despotism was trenching upon liberty, no such cry was heard as that of any danger to the Church. But no sooner did the tide appear to turn; no sooner have liberty and knowledge appeared to be beginning to flow in, than the cry of 'danger to the Church,' has, in almost every instance begun to resound.

As it will thus be found that this cry has in almost all ages and countries been a mischievous cry, so it will almost always and every where be found that it has been the cry, not of the whole of the church, but only of a part, and that of a part by no means considerable in point of numbers, but forward and capable of making a great noise; which, by the silence and non-resistance of the greater number, is too frequently and too naturally mistaken for the voice of the whole.

As friends to the Lancasterian plan for educating the poor, it is our most earnest desire to have no controversy with any religious class of our countrymen, of whom it is our object to combine all classes in a grand project of national good. The Lancasterian plans count among their most zealous and effectual supporters not a few of the most sincere and steadfast followers and members of the church, both lay and clerical; and we doubt not that every day will add to their numbers, when the sophistry with which it is at present endeavoured to oppose them is refuted, and the affected apprehensions of evil are shown for what they are, and well known and understood by the public.

But unfortunately the name of the Church has been converted into an engine of war against us. In the use which is thus made of it, we are in self-defence constrained to resist it. But we desire at the outset, that what is extorted from us in opposition to their own proceedings, by an ambitious, a clamorous and political section of churchmen, may not be construed (as it seems to be the wish to construe every thing) into an opposition to the Establishment as such. Such friends of the establishment as see to the bottom of this important case, will see that the men who are doing injury to the church, are the men who, either led by the most anile bigotry, or in pursuance of their own ends, seek to stake the name and credit of the church upon the defeat of a scheme so clearly for the benefit of mankind, that in an age like the present it is hardly possible that it should fail of success.

The circumstances of this case are pretty notorious. Whatever may be the nature of the institutions provided in England for the education of the higher orders of the people, no general provision whatsoever has been made for the education of the poor. In other protestant countries, as in Scotland, at Geneva, in Switzerland, and Holland, the education of the lower orders was regarded as an object of the greatest importance, both in a religious and a political point of view. Careful provision was made for it. Parochial schools were established; funds were set apart for their maintenance; means for acquiring the first and most important parts of the literary branch of education were placed within the reach of all the people; all the people were actually taught them; and the lower orders, in all these several countries, as they have been the best educated, so have they been the most virtuous and orderly that ever existed upon the face of the earth. In England the case was widely different. The education of the lower orders was totally neglected. In general they could neither write nor read. The formation of their minds was the result of chance; that is to say, of the casual and disorderly circumstances in which they were placed. It is true that they still exhibited a number of virtues, which the political circumstances of the country happily engendered. But the political circumstances of the country received not, as they ought to have received, any assistance from the education of the people; they suffered, on the other hand, all the disadvantages which the non-education of the people carried in such numbers in its bosom.

The hideous deformity of this picture, of an ignorant and brutal people in an enlightened age and country, began at last to strike with commiseration the eyes of philanthropic and public-spirited individuals; and means began to be thought of for extending to the people, as in other protestant countries, the blessings of education. It is now considerably more than half a century since charity schools, almost all supported by private contributions, began to be erected; and in some few parishes, where the inhabitants were wealthy, means were provided for educating a small proportion of the children of the poor, in general a very small proportion even in those parishes where the schools existed; while the children of the poor throughout the rest of the country remained deprived of all the means of education.

At this point the business rested. During a period of fifty years, the education of the poor received little extension. A few thousands in the metropolis, and a similar proportion in a few more of the more opulent towns in England, might be found receiving the rudiments of learning. The rest of the people were abandoned to their own tuition; and that in a country boasting that it was the richest and the most enlightened country in the universe.

At last an individual arose, who, having proved by his own experience that the most useful branches of education might be taught to the poor at a wonderfully small expense, at an expense so small that even the strength of private contributions might rise equal to the demand for the whole nation, conceived the glorious design of extending the benefits of education to every member of the community. While bishops and archbishops, and deans and rectors, and lords and gentlemen, looked on in apathy, this individual performed two things: he first proved that the education of the poor might be rendered incredibly cheap; he next conceived the truly great and magnanimous idea of rousing by his own exertions a sufficient number of individuals in the nation to contribute the expense which the education of the whole body of the people would require. This, be it observed, is what Joseph Lancaster did alone. In this merit no one dares venture to claim a share with him. While the Dr Bells and the Dr Marshes,[20] the Bishop *As* and the Bishop *Bs*, enjoyed their tranquillity and their ease, without an effort for the education of the poor, without a single school to which their exertions gave birth, Mr Lancaster proved, by experiment on a large scale, that education for the poor might be rendered incredibly cheap; that thus the means of carrying it on to the requisite extent might with comparative ease be procured; and he conceived the noble resolution of rousing the nation at large to afford those means. Aware how often attempts had been made, and by men much more powerful than himself, and made in vain, to obtain a share of the *public* funds for the maintenance of a system, co-extensive with the nation, of education for the poor, he conceived the *new* idea of rendering *private* funds equal to the great national work. He *demonstrated* by his grand experiment the practicability of the scheme; and he called upon the nation to join him in giving it execution and reality. To the honour of the nation be it spoken, to the honour of Him who has so long stood at its head, and of many of those who are the nearest to him in dignity and influence, the call was heard with an attention and sensibility greater than could have been expected. Universal interest seemed to be excited. Schools were multiplied. Men seemed to be astonished at the facility with which the elements of learning might be universally imparted. To the zeal and enthusiasm of a Philanthropist, Mr Lancaster happily added the greatest activity, fearlessness, and perseverance. New schools seemed ready to spring up in every part of the country. But when things were in this situation, the cry that 'the Church was in danger' became suddenly loud.

The leading facts are shortly these; and they are speaking facts; men will not fail to attend to them. During upwards of fifty years that ignorance reigned triumphant, save for the slight and disproportionate resistance afforded by the charity and Sunday schools, who ever cried that there was any danger to the church? During the century or centuries which preceded, and in which the reign of ignorance was complete, who ever cried that there was any danger to the church? A time arrives, when it appears that education is to become general; and then comes the cry that 'the church is in danger!'

What appears from this at first sight seems to be;—1. That in the opinion of the authors of the cry, Ignorance is *not* dangerous to the church;—2. That Knowledge *is* dangerous to the church.

What appears with indubitable certainty is;—that ignorance in their opinion is neither dangerous to the church nor disagreeable to the clergy; because, were it dangerous to the church, the hierarchy would certainly during the long period of its reign have set up the cry of danger; and had it been disagreeable to themselves, they would most certainly have exerted themselves, as Lancaster has exerted himself, and with ten thousand times his effect, (for what is the influence of ten thousand Lancasters to the influence of the clergy?) to extirpate the ignorance by the force of education, and to plant knowledge in its stead.

If the authors, however, of the cry say that they do *not* hold knowledge to be dangerous to the church, that they do not hold it dangerous in one of its modes, viz. when communicated by themselves, though they *do* hold it dangerous in all other possible modes,—be it so: they shall have the advantage of every thing they choose to assume, as far as they and their assumptions can bear one another out. The assumption too, in the present case, is a pretty remarkable one; we leave the import of it to be weighed by others. It is, however, certain, that if they do not think knowledge dangerous to the church, they at least think it *useless*; because, did they not think so, they would infallibly have done what was in their power (and every thing to this purpose was in their power) to render education universal from one end of the kingdom to the other. Having not done what was in their power, they must confess that they either looked upon education as useless; or that, knowing it to be useful, it was not suitable to their interest or inclination to do what depended upon them for its establishment; that though they knew it to be useful, and had it in their power to render it universal, they did no such thing.

But it is high time to demand of those who cry 'church-danger!' what it is they would be at? They must cease talking in the air. Let them speak specifically and pointedly. What is it they wish?

The children of the poor are observed to be in general

brought up without education, abandoned to themselves, in the streets and in the fields, learning all the idle and disorderly habits which render men bad members of society. A Dissenter, be it observed, is the man who steps forward and says, 'It is possible to dry up this flood of evil by applying a remedy to the source. I will show how it may be done. I call upon the nation to second me. And if they second me with but very trifling efforts, we shall infallibly accomplish the purpose.'

Now what happened? The children going without education were the children of churchmen and dissenters mixed; but the children of churchmen in by far the greatest proportion; for it is a notorious fact that the dissenters are in general solicitous about the education of their children; and of the totally uneducated part of the people, almost the whole belongs to the church. This is a fact which ought not to be lost sight of in this question. It is so notoriously true, that we should not suppose any one would venture to contradict it. What then was Mr Lancaster, when he conceived a scheme for educating by voluntary contribution the whole of the uneducated poor, to do? Was he to limit the advantages of his plan to the children of dissenters, and shut his doors upon the children of churchmen? In that case, a different clamour would have been raised against him. What illiberality, it would have been said, what malignity is this! What have the children of churchmen done that they should be excluded from any of the benefits of the improvements of education? This would have been an accusation of weight, because it would have been just and founded on utility.

Such narrow plans suited not the views of those who wished to see the whole of the people educated. Mr

Lancaster opened his doors to all denominations of Christians equally. It is evident that this he could do upon one condition only; viz. his not teaching Christianity to the children upon a plan different from that of which their parents, or those on whom they depended, approved. There were two ways by which this obstacle to the general education of the poor could be avoided, and only two. The one was to abstain from teaching Christianity altogether; teaching reading and writing separately from it, just in the same way as painting, or music, or mathematics, are taught separately from Christianity, without any supposed injury to it. The other mode of avoiding this obstacle was,—to teach so much of Christianity, and so much only, as all Christians were agreed about. This fortunately was the principal part; for it was the Holy Scriptures; held to be the full and sufficient rule of faith and practice by all denominations of protestant Christians; a rule too, which by all protestants, as distinguished from catholics, is held to be so plain and clear, that every ordinary Christian who can read it may see its meaning, and is in no danger of risking his salvation by mistaking its meaning. This latter mode of avoiding the obstacle to the dissemination of education was what Mr Lancaster adopted; and he hoped that thereby he might obviate every objection. Without such a plan he must have contented himself with teaching a few children, while the streets around him swarmed with others presenting the most urgent demand for instruction, which there was no one who appeared disposed to afford them. By adopting this seemingly unobjectionable plan, he was enabled to give the most important instruction to all.

But Mr Lancaster was very much mistaken when he

imagined that his plan would not be objected to. It has been railed against, as a scheme, if not intended, at any rate calculated, to extirpate Christianity. It has even been broadly and unblushingly asserted in a high church quarter*, that Mr Lancaster, as being a Quaker, is *no Christian*; Quakers being *not Christians*, by reason they do not celebrate with outward symbols Baptism and the Lord's Supper. But even by more moderate antagonists it has been asserted, that to teach children to read, and even to train them in habits of reading the Bible, unless adherence to a particular creed be inculcated upon them along with it, is to train them to renounce Christianity. This opinion, however, the most intelligent and discerning part of the Lancasterian opponents have dropt. Dr Herbert Marsh was knowing enough to stand clear of it.

Dr Marsh, and those who are as knowing as Dr Marsh, take a different ground. They do not say that teaching the children to read, and accustoming them to read the Bible, (leaving out the teaching of any particular creed,) is the way to extirpate Christianity. But they say, that teaching children to read, and accustoming them to read the Bible, without inculcating the particular creed of the Church of England, is the way to extirpate the Church of England.

There are two accusations, then, against which the Lancasterian scheme of educating the poor is called upon to find an answer. The first is, that it is inimical to Christianity. The second is, that it is inimical to the Church of England. We shall state what appear to us to be the facts relative to both points.

1. First, then, we are to notice the accusation, that teaching the poor to read, and habituating them to read

* See Antijacobin Review.[21]

the Bible, without inculcating any particular creed, is the way to make them renounce Christianity.

'The not inculcating some particular creed,' is the main spring of the objection. But it is to be remembered, that by the supposition, the children educated in Lancaster's schools would otherwise not have been at school at all; they would have had neither creed nor any thing else inculcated upon them*. The two cases to be compared are the cases of non-education entirely, and the case of education in one of the Lancasterian schools. In the non-inculcation of any particular creed, it is observable that both are upon a level; both are equal. The question then is, Whether the non-inculcation of a creed accompanied with total ignorance, or the non-inculcation of a creed, accompanied with the talent of reading and the knowledge of the Bible, be the most likely to lead to the renunciation of Christianity? More concisely, the question is, Whether knowledge or ignorance be most favourable to the belief of Christianity? Those who really disbelieve Christianity may hold to the latter, and with consistency; those who really believe Christianity must, without the grossest inconsistency, resolutely maintain the former. All those who believe in Christianity must therefore allow that Lancaster's schools are favourable to Christianity, as much as knowledge is favourable to it, and ignorance unfavourable.

This argument we regard as perfectly conclusive and unanswerable. However, the grand object of teaching to read and write deserves to be examined a little more closely by itself. We cannot—viewing the matter on all its sides, and examining it with the most anxious

* The supposed case of education in supposed schools of the Church of England will immediately be considered by itself.

attention—we cannot see that it would be any detriment to Christianity, if teaching to read and write should be deemed one part of education, and teaching Christianity another. Reading and writing are one thing; Christianity is another thing. Christianity is just as different from reading and writing, as it is from chemistry or mathematics. It would be just as reasonable to blame Mr Davy[22] for not teaching Church of England creed along with his chemistry, as to blame Mr Lancaster for not teaching Church of England creed along with his reading and writing. What is to hinder Mr Lancaster and his pupils from teaching to read and write, and the clergy of the Church of England from teaching their creed, with all the industry and skill of which they are capable? We will point out to them a plan, by which they may certainly do for their creed all that they can desire. Let the clergyman of each parish employ regularly the evening of the Sunday in inculcating Church of England creed upon the children of his parishioners. He may easily have, if he chooses it, a list of all the children in his parish. Let him assemble them together, and teach them with as much industry his religion, as Mr Lancaster teaches them reading and writing. Thus will the teaching of religion and the teaching of reading and writing, though in different hands, go on with equal success; and if the division of labour be here, as it is found in other provinces of education, an improvement, religion as well as reading and writing will thus be better taught, when taught separately, than if they were taught in conjunction. Let the pastor of each parish be, as it behoves him to be, and as he is paid for being, the teacher of religion to the *young* as well as to the old. Let the teacher of reading and writing be he who can do it best; and let him keep his religion entirely to himself*. This seems a rational plan for accomplishing all purposes. For the clergy to object to reading and writing, because it is not Christianity, is just to object to one good thing because it is not another good thing. If the clergy, however, go about objecting to allow men's teaching reading and writing, under pretence of anxiety for the teaching of Christianity, while they themselves to whom it peculiarly belongs to teach Christianity take no steps for doing what it is evident they might so easily do to teach Christianity in the most effectual manner to the children of their parishioners, their zeal, it is evident, goes no further than words, it is effectual to no purpose but evil. It is effectual to *prevent* good, viz. the teaching of reading and writing; but it is altogether ineffectual to *do* good, viz. to make the clergy take upon themselves the truly apostolical and religious task of teaching the children of their parishioners their religious creed in separate assemblies each Sunday.

What has enabled the alarmists to confound this most important practical distinction, between the teaching of Christianity, and teaching the mechanical faculties of reading and writing, is the ambiguity and uncertainty of language; that grand instrument of deception, both when men deceive themselves and when they want to deceive others. 'An education without religion!' cry our opponents: 'What an anti-christian idea! Come, Christians, we entreat you, and assist us in exploding it.' Before joining in this exhortation, we have one short question to which we should wish to receive an answer. Who recommends 'education without religion?' Not certainly the Lancasterians. Education, it is to be observed, in its due latitude, is a very comprehensive

* That is, as far as his school is concerned.

word. It means, in fact, all that the child and the youth learns that is useful for the purposes of life, from the moment of birth to the time when he is fit to become his own master, and have the charge of his own actions. Who recommends that this period of life should pass without religious instruction? The Lancasterians, at any rate, wish that it should receive as much as possible of religious instruction. And assuredly they do nothing to prevent it. Every considerate man will determine how much what they do is calculated to favour it.

If it be asked, why they do not add a particular course of religious instruction to that of reading and writing, the answer is obvious—It is impossible. A plan to teach reading and writing in the most effectual manner to the poor, must be a plan calculated to admit them on the easiest terms. Teach the children only reading and writing, and you may teach the whole children of a populous city in one school. Add to this a religious creed, and you must then have many schools; one for every denomination of Christians. Would not this be to render the teaching of reading and writing to the poor many times more expensive? In other words, would not this be to render it impracticable? Is the insisting, then, upon the adding a religious creed to the teaching of reading and writing, any other thing than insisting that reading and writing shall not be taught to the poor? It is in effect the very same thing. It is possible that those who so insist have not hitherto seen that it is the same thing. But what is impossible is, that any body should have it pointed out to him, and not instantly recognise that it is so. As we trust that the whole nation will speedily have it pointed out to them, we shall then have a test which will exhibit to all men, who is in earnest for the teaching of reading and writing to the poor; who is in earnest for the prevention of it, with whatever show of friendship to it he may be cloking his designs.

It is abundantly evident, that what is to be done for the poor voluntarily and extensively, must be done cheaply. It is equally evident, that in almost all cases, what is to be done the most cheaply, ought to be done upon the largest possible scale. In few cases will this be found to hold to a greater degree than in the teaching to read and write. To add religious creeds to this teaching would render a multitude of small schools necessary, where a few large ones would suffice; would, in short, demand an expense which the circumstances of the case render unattainable; that is to say, render the teaching of the poor to read and write a thing impracticable. This is the end to which the cry about their creed, of a party pretending to represent the clergy and the church, naturally conducts. The world will judge of its desirableness.

Suppose, when the calamities of a season of scarcity suggested to benevolent minds the expedient of soup-institutions, that instead of one large institution for a whole town or district, to which the poor were admitted indiscriminately, a number of small ones had been rendered necessary, one for each creed; and that no soup had been given but in conjunction with an appropriate creed,—would it have been possible to extend the relief by which so much misery was prevented, to one half the number of sufferers, who, when the operation was performed on the largest scale, and the poor were admitted indiscriminately, partook of the benefit? That it was just as possible to unite a creed to eating on charity, as it is to the learning to read and write on charity, will be denied by nobody.

It is by an accidental association merely that learning

the principles of religion has been thought to be more necessarily connected with the learning to read and write, than with any other mechanical talent. Why should not that still more essential branch of education, the teaching children to *speak*, be required to be accompanied with the inculcation of a creed, just as much as the teaching children to read and write? Where is the difference? What is the learning to read and write? Is it any thing else than the becoming acquainted with *written* discourse? as the learning to speak is the becoming acquainted with *spoken* discourse. The last is the principal thing: the former is only a contrivance for giving permanence to the latter. If it be said that at the tender age when children learn to speak, they cannot understand the principles of religion; we believe it may with equal certainty be affirmed, that at the age when it is proposed to teach them reading, they are equally incapable of understanding the principles of religion. A child at four, five, six, and seven years of age is just as incapable of annexing any rational ideas to the terms God, Salvation, Trinity, &c. as a child at two or three; and a child at two or three is just as capable of being made to repeat a few words by rote as at six or seven; and as far as the annexing reverential feelings to the repetition of certain words is reckoned a good, the sooner the association is begun the better. In point of fact, indeed, experience is on our side; for pious and careful mothers, we believe, have in general taught their children to repeat a short prayer, and to answer a few religious questions, as, Who made them? Who redeemed them? &c. before they have begun to read, and as soon as ever they can speak.

2. The second accusation to which we shall advert, is,—that teaching children to read and write, without

teaching them the Church of England creed, is the way to make them renounce the Church of England.

We believe that no sentence more condemnatory of the Church of England ever was pronounced, or can be pronounced by her most declared enemies, than is thus pronounced by her professing votaries. For, what does it import? That if men are rendered intelligent, and left without any bias, the religion of the Church of England is that which they are sure not to adopt. Is this a conclusion which they who maintain the premises are willing to avow? Far from it. But there is only one way by which they can evade it; and when men are hard pushed, and driven to the wall, they will adopt very awkward means of defence. One assertion there is, and but one, which they can make use of. It is an assertion totally unfounded. But what of that? Assertion with most people is taken for proof: and at the very worst, assertion always affords an image of defence, and avoids the humiliating acknowledgement of defeat.

The assertion is,—that *not* to give a bias to the Church of England creed, *is* to give a bias to other creeds. It does appear to us, however, that this implies the very same stigma upon the Church of England creed, as the proposition considered in the former sentence. It implies, that if the Church of England creed is left on even ground with other creeds; if pains are not taken to give it the earliest advantages over other creeds, men will in general disdain and reject it.

If it be the intention to insinuate, that in schools in which pains are not taken to give the advantages to the Church of England creed, pains will be taken to give the advantages to other creeds, this, with regard to the Lancasterian schools, is totally false. There is not the smallest ground for the imputation. Never was there a surmise more thoroughly gratuitous; more completely invented for the sake of the purpose in the service of which it is applied; more totally at variance with the facts of the case.

In these schools the fact most assuredly is, that no advantages are given to any one creed over another. It is evident to whoever has eyes not blinded by prejudice, wherewith to see, that no object naturally can be nearer to the heart of Mr Lancaster than to treat in his school all creeds with the most exact and scrupulous equality. His very enemies allow that he is an enthusiast for the education of the poor; that he wishes to see them taught, and to be the instrument of teaching them, to the greatest extent; universally, if possible. But to meddle with the creeds of the children in his schools; to afford advantages to one creed, disadvantages to another, would be the most obvious and infallible course to drive the children from his schools; to defeat his own most darling purpose. The only plan, upon which he can so much as hope to carry that purpose into execution, is that of treating creeds with absolute and perfect equality; that so the children of no class of Christians may be deterred from resorting to his schools. If then a man's strongest passion be allowed to constitute his strongest interest; and if a man's strongest interest afford the strongest security for his conduct, the public has the strongest security of which human affairs admit, that Mr Lancaster will observe strict equality towards all creeds in the teaching of reading and writing.

Nor is this all. There is, moreover, the evidence of facts. Of the thousands of children to whom Mr Lancaster has taught reading and writing, it is not known that so much as one has adopted his religious creed. One fact is remarkable: of all the youths of whom he has made choice to train for masters, not one has been distinguished as being of his own religious persuasion. Can there be a stronger proof than this? Considering the cry that has been set up, what is truly remarkable is, that of these selected youths the greater part have belonged to the Church of England; and while under the tuition of Mr Lancaster, and boarded and lodged in his house, regularly attended (and attend) divine service in the parish church.

Another thing which is well worthy of attention is, that the sect of Christians to whom Mr Lancaster belongs are exempt from the spirit of proselyting. It makes no part either of their principles or practice. Nothing can be more unfounded than the surmise, that any bias is given in favour of any creed more than another in the Lancasterian schools.

To say then, that to teach, as in the Lancasterian schools, reading and writing, acting towards the Church of England creed in all possible respects exactly as toward other creeds, is in these schools to give a bias against the Church of England, is neither more nor less than to say that to give mental culture is to give a bias against the Church of England. As this, however, is a conclusion which the persons who cry 'There is danger to the church' are concerned in interest not to avow, so they are sure not to avow, but to cloke it up and hide it by all possible means. Those, however, who are concerned to see things, not as they are masked and habited for the purposes of particular persons, but as they are in themselves, it behoves and imports to strip off such masks, that they may not be rendered the dupes of artificial and false appearances.

There is in this case, considering the country and the age, something, it is evident, exceedingly remarkable.

Let not any part of the clergy of the Church of England attempt to disguise the disgraceful fact, that the children of the poor belonging to that church are untaught. Let it be imprinted in the memory of every one, that in the idea of the Lancasterian scheme this is essentially included; for, if the children of the poor of the Church of England are taught, there is, as far as the church is concerned, nothing to be done by the Lancasterians, nothing to be dreaded by the church. Where schools are provided by the church for the children of her poor, as good as are provided for the poor of all denominations by the Lancasterians, there will always be a motive to a member of the Church of England to send his children to the school of his own church; a motive which when the balance is equal will infallibly turn the scale.

It is the untaught part, therefore, of the children of the poor of the Church of England who are in any danger of coming to the Lancasterian schools; those who, without these schools, must go without teaching. Left to themselves, those unfortunate children have the Church of England creed as little impressed upon them surely, in the streets and in the fields, as in the Lancasterian schools. In the streets and in the fields, however, they have implanted in them the seeds of vice and profligacy. In the Lancasterian schools they are trained in all those habits which are the foundation of virtue and worth. In point of Church of England creed, the two cases are exactly equal. In every other respect, it is scarcely possible to conceive any case more desirable than the one, more undesirable than the other.

What the portion who oppose us of the clergy of the Church of England, therefore, by their present conduct declare, is—that they would rather see, as they have hitherto seen, the children of the poor belonging to their church brought up in the streets and in the fields, where no creed is taught, but ignorance is retained and vice engendered; than see them in the schools of Lancaster, where no creed indeed is taught, but where reading and writing are taught, and where those habits are acquired, of industry, attention, orderliness, &c. on which good conduct in life depends. There are, indeed, propositions too repugnant to the sentiments of mankind to bear to be avowed; and this is one of them. But our countrymen should look not merely to words. Words are at the command of any man. Let them look to actions. Let the testimony which *they* yield be that to which the chief attention is directed.

Let us suppose, for a moment, that the fact really were what it is not. Let us put the case, that children were to receive a bias against the Church of England in the Lancasterian schools, and that not partially only, or even generally; let us go to the extravagant length of saying universally. Is there really in any quarter (we hope there is not) so much of shamelessness existing, as to say that it would be better for the country that its poor should grow up ignorant, vicious, profligate Church of England men, than intelligent, orderly, virtuous Dissenters?

Is Church of England creed so great a virtue, as to counterbalance ignorance and all degrees of vice? Is Dissenters' creed so great a vice as to counterbalance knowledge and all degrees of virtue? Is the most worthless Church of England man a more valuable member of society than the most meritorious Dissenter?

Let us suppose, on the other hand, that every ignorant and worthless Church of England man could be converted into an intelligent and virtuous Dissenter; would not the nation be a prodigious gainer?

Our enemies will not say that Church of England creed is better than intelligence and virtue; they will not say that Dissenters' creed is worse than ignorance and vice; but their hypothesis requires that it *should be* said, implies that it *is* said; and they endeavour to bring proof of their hypothesis.

The proof they bring may well indeed be regarded as extraordinary. It consists of two things. The one is, a profanation and perversion of religion: the other is, a false and most mischievous principle of politics. The first consists in making religion an engine of state: the second consists in asserting that a religious engine is good for the support of government. Of these ingredients the argument is made up in the following manner. It is asserted, and without any hesitation or blushing, that the Church of England is necessary for the support of the British constitution; that the British constitution, though the best, and for that reason the most steadfast, of all forms of government, could not stand without the support of the Church of England; that, therefore, in order to support the constitution, Church of England creed, though attended with worthlessness, ought to be preferred to Dissenters' creed, though accompanied with merit.

1. The first of the propositions included in this argument is, that religion is, in England, very convenient to be converted into an engine of state. That to make of religion an engine of state is a profanation of religion, and leads by necessary consequence to its corruption, is, we believe, agreed among all the best and purest theologians of all persuasions. What reason says on the case is indeed not obscure. It is of the nature of an engine to be twisted and turned to suit the purposes of that of which it is made the engine. For clergymen then

to point out religion to kings and statesmen, as an instrument of which they may make use for state purposes, is to point out religion as a thing that may be twisted and turned, and modelled and fashioned, to answer the purposes of statesmen. That this is *practical* irreligion, there can be no manner of doubt. It is making of religion a secondary thing to politics; that is, to the interests of the men who happen, for the time being, to be vested with the powers of the state. This, it cannot be disputed, is *practically* to deny its divine original.

To prove that religion is thus deeply injured by converting it into an engine of state, we shall not content ourselves with our own authority, nor with the authority of reason. Those are weak. We shall have recourse to the authority of a clergyman of the Church of England; an authority which seems to unite every thing in its favour. It is not the authority of an ancient divine, whose opinions might seem antiquated; nor of an enthusiast, whose opinions might appear the offspring of a heated imagination; nor of a man indifferent to the preservation either of the Church of England, or of the British constitution, but of a warm friend to both; not of a weak man, but of a man whom the Church of England counts among the most enlightened and philosophical of her sons. The man of whom we speak is Dr Paley;[23] who, in that work of his which the late Mr Windham,[24] in the House of Commons, declared to contain nothing but the quintessence of wisdom from beginning to end, thus expresses himself:

'The authority of a church establishment is founded in its utility: and whenever, upon this principle, we deliberate concerning the form, propriety, or comparative excellency of different establishments, the *single* view under which we ought to consider any of them is that of a *scheme of instruction*; the *single* end we ought to propose by them is, the preservation and communication of *religious knowledge*. Every other idea and every other end that have been mixed with this, as the making of the church an engine, or even an *ally*, of the state; converting it into the means of strengthening or diffusing influence; or regarding it as a support of regal in opposition to popular forms of government, have served only to debase the institution, and to introduce into it numerous corruptions and abuses.' This important passage the reader will find in Paley's Principles of Moral and Political Philosophy, book vi. chapter 10, page 305 of the 2nd vol. fifth edition, printed, London, 1788.—After this we trust we shall not hear that there is danger in letting the children of the poor be taught reading and writing in the Lancasterian schools, *because the church is necessary to support the constitution*; because the church is 'the engine or the ally of the state:' for all honest men, with Dr Paley at their head, will be ready to cry,—This is only 'to debase the institutions of religion; to introduce into them numerous corruptions and abuses.'

2. The next observation which we made upon this ecclesiastical argument was, that it involved one of the most false and mischievous principles that ever were applied to the corruption of the science or practice of government.

The principle is, that religion is a good engine to be employed for the use and support of civil government.

As far as government is grounded on the principle of utility, it supports itself. It neither needs any other support; nor will it ever look out for any. To this, reason and experience bear united testimony. Two things, and two things only, are necessary to the support of government. 1. That it should conduct on the principle of general utility the affairs of the community; and 2. That the people as a body should see and know that it does so. If the first of these is done, the last is easily accomplished; a little pains in the way of instruction, when people are interested in really seeing things as they are, and when they are competent to see them as they are, seldom fail, and can never long fail, completely to answer the purpose.

To teach governments therefore to look out for extraneous supports, is exactly to teach them to neglect their real and intrinsic supports. These are two, 1st, Governing well; and 2dly, Instructing the people, so as to make them understand that they are well governed. To teach governments, as is too frequently done, to look to religion for support, is to encourage bad government as far as that support is depended upon. Religion is no further wanted to the support of any government than as far as that government is bad. To persuade therefore any government that it may to any degree depend upon the support of religion, is just to persuade the rulers, that to that same degree they may safely govern ill.

Dr Paley has informed us above, that 'the alliance of church and state' never takes place but to the corruption of religion. It is equally certain that it never takes place but to the corruption of government. It comes to afford protection to misrule. As far as it is seen to have power, so far it is seen that bad government may be practised and be safe. As far as it is seen that bad government may be practised and be safe, both reason and experience lead us to conclude that it will be practised. The alliance of church and state is then, literally and strictly, even to the last atom, the alliance of religious abuse and corruption with political abuse and corruption. The chain of proof is here as close, unbroken, and infallible, as any that contingent affairs admit of. To teach rulers how far they may depend upon religion for their support, is merely to teach them how far they may neglect or betray their duty; how far the interests of the community at large may be sacrificed to the interests of their rulers. That this doctrine has been industriously and successfully preached with a view to profit by the abuses to which it gives rise, the history of ecclesiastical usurpation in many countries affords the most wonderful and the most instructive examples.

It thus appears, and with extraordinary force of evidence, that the clerical argument waged with so much zeal and outcry in opposition to the Lancasterian scheme of educating the poor, depends upon principles the most odious and mischievous which it is possible to conceive; principles which lead to nothing but the grossest corruption of both religion and government. Both church and state, therefore, are interested, and that deeply, in renouncing and disclaiming them; and, along with them, the argument which depends upon them for its whole support.

Something more is yet to be said on the support which it is pretended that governments may receive from religion. We suppose that few words will be necessary to prove that nowadays that support is but small. Men understand the nature of religion, and the nature of government, better now than they did in the days when governments received so much support and suffered so much oppression from religion. We have learned above from Dr Paley, that 'the authority of a church is founded solely upon its utility *to religion*;' that in so far only as it is *religiously useful*, are men concerned to have a church establishment, or ought to have one. Who would have dared to *talk*, who would have been enlightened enough to *think* about the church in this manner three centuries ago? But if the authority of a church establishment rests solely upon its utility, so, unquestionably, does that of government. This men now understand. There is no superstition now in the case. There is little of blind, unthinking, unfounded reverence any where. Utility is what men look out for. No advice therefore can be more treacherous, in the present state of knowledge, than to encourage governments to depend upon religion. As sure as it is depended upon by any government in any part of the world, so sure is the fall of the throne, if not of the altar, preparing; and the more enlightened the people, and the greater this unwise dependence, the nearer unquestionably will be the ruin.

A government depending upon religion! That is to say, a government *not* depending upon its own excellence, and upon the instruction which it gives to the people; a government which has either not excellence on which to depend, or which is afraid or regardless of the instruction of the people. In the days of ignorance and barbarity, true! the support of religion to the worst of governments was then a power that might be depended upon. The human mind was in that age weak, and deluded, and fearful. It knew little of the true nature of either religion or government. Now a good deal is known of both; and if they are seen any where uniting together for their mutual perversion, for the creation or maintenance of religious and political abuses, (and the nature of the case denies that they can unite for any other purpose*,) they will not by that means perpetuate the abuses; they will only in most instances bring upon them a violent and precipitate end. This is not theory. The world has during the last fifty years been reading the most remarkable practical lessons on the subjects. If any government can now trust any part of its salvation to religion, it must be indeed infatuated. If it were not visible to all men, in the present enlightened state of the world, that such alliance of church with state is a perversion of religion, Dr Paley has told it them. The perversion and abuse of religion will go a little way, in the present state of men's minds, to satisfy them for the want of good government; to make them submit to abuses; which, be it ever remembered, is the sole political purpose to which the support of religion, as an engine of state, is applicable.

It is very remarkable that the wretched *dictum* of a weak and contemptible king should have had as much influence in the government of England, as it certainly has had from his to the present day! 'No bishop, no king,' said James the First, who allowed himself to be called the second Solomon. What *he* meant by king, all the world knows. He meant *despot*. 'No bishop, no despot.' In this proposition there may be all the truth which James imagined. Despotism is political abuse: to this, extraneous supports are absolutely necessary; and so long as people are ignorant enough not to see through

* If it be urged that an established church implies such union, and that this argument, therefore, bears against all establishments, —we answer, It is evident that Dr Paley thought not so; for the argument, as far as the perversion of religion is concerned, is his. That an Institute maintained for securing religious instruction and access to religious ordinances to the people, *need* not have any connexion with the politics of the state, we should think were too evident to demand illustration.

the perversion of religion, religion may afford the best and strongest support of despotism. But what have we to do with that? The British constitution is not a system of abuses, which cannot depend upon its own utility, and the discernment and intelligence of the people! And, besides, Dr Paley has told us 'that the church can never be made an engine, or even an ally, of the state; can never be converted into the means of strengthening or diffusing influence; or regarded as a support of regal in opposition to popular forms of government, without being debased as a religious institution, without having introduced into it numerous corruptions and abuses*.' Those who preach up this debasement and corruption of the church for the sake of defeating the Lancasterian schemes for the education of the poor, are thus seen to pursue the worst of ends by the very worst of means. The proceeding is mischievous throughout. Where it is not attended with evil consciousness and evil intention, the delusion must be gross and pitiable. Where it is attended with evil consciousness and evil intention, no proceeding certainly was ever more profligate and depraved.

We may now advert to another argument. If the church be unfit to be supported as an engine or ally of the state, it is at any rate, it may be said, highly necessary to support it for the maintenance of religion. This is a proposition which we do not mean to controvert. We wage no war with the establishment. Whether an establishment be conducive or not conducive to the good of religion, is a controverted point: the world is divided about it, and has been for ages. Men with the very best intentions towards their species have taken both sides of the question. It is a controversy far too

* See above, pp. 142–3.

wide for the limits of such a publication as ours; neither is it necessary for the purpose in hand that we should at all meddle with it.

All that we wish to have distinctly defined and understood is, the doctrine of Dr Paley—viz. that a church establishment, if useful, is useful only to *religious* purposes; is in no degree useful for *political* purposes; never can be taken and used as a *political* support, 'without debasement, without corruption and abuse.'

Now what we have to say to this new argument is—that the education of the poor in the Lancasterian schools never can do any injury to the church *in the religious point of view*. We regard this as a most important part of the subject in controversy; and we hope it will be well considered, and the conclusions carefully remembered.

Of the children growing up in the streets and in the fields, without instruction in goodness of any sort, but with the instruction and practice of wickedness, suppose that every one were taken and educated in Lancaster's schools, and rendered a dissenter. Would this be to the detriment of *religion*? Would not many more, to a certainty, become religious men under this tuition, than amid the profligate habits acquired in the streets? If so, then religion would be promoted by the Lancasterian schools. The very end which the church has in view, the sole end for which it ought to exist, would be carried on by the Lancasterian schools. The Lancasterian schools would be the auxiliary, the coadjutor of the church.

The true object of a religious establishment, as it is viewed by Dr Paley, and by all rational and distinterested men, is—not that all men should become of the establishment, but that all men should be *religious*. The reason of an establishment, says Dr Paley, is founded upon this, that if religion were left to be supported by the voluntary attachment of men, it would be neglected; men would abandon religion; religion would be lost. But on the other hand, it is on these principles of Dr Paley abundantly plain, that if men would be religious without an establishment, the reason for establishments would no longer remain. An establishment exists, not for the sake of those who would be religious without it, but for the sake of those who would *not* be religious without it. It upholds religious ordinances, and disseminates religious instruction for the benefit of those who would be too careless about religion to provide those advantages for themselves; and who, by their growth and multiplication, it is feared, might in time go far to the extinction of religion.

When men become religious, then, though not exactly according to the forms of an establishment, the *end* of the establishment is nevertheless attained, as much as if they belonged to the establishment. The end of the establishment is, that the members of the community should be religious: Well, by the supposition, the men in question are religious: Therefore the object of the establishment is gained. Whatever is done, out of the establishment, to render men religious, is done in aid of the purposes of the establishment. What is opposite to the establishment is not religion; religion, though more or less diversified in form, is concurrent with the establishment; it is only *irreligion* that is opposed to it. If the object and end of the establishment be, as Dr Paley says, religion solely, not politics, the multiplication of dissenters is no injury to the church. The end for the sake of which the church is established, is equally gained; only it is gained by some diversity of means.

If it be said, that of all religions, the religion of the establishment is the most conducive to the salvation of men; this, it is evident, is so very disputed a point, that no practical regulation can with reason or propriety be founded upon it. If any religion leads to a breach of legal obligations, it is within the control of the civil magistrate. If any religion is inferior to that of the church in its conformity to reason and scripture, this may be made to appear; and if it is made to appear, men, when well instructed, will be sure to quit the worse religion for the better. This follows undeniably from the principle that religion is founded upon reason; and is no better than superstition as far as it is founded upon any thing else. What the clergy of the church then have to do, as often as they perceive a religion less conformable than their own to reason and scripture, is—to exert themselves, by exposition and argument, to make that disconformity appear. They will thus hardly ever fail to do one of two things. They will either purify and amend the exceptionable religion, by inducing its votaries to render it more conformable to scripture and reason; or they will gain them over from their inferior religion to the better religion of the church. This is the duty which by their situation an established clergy are called upon to perform. In this manner they do good to those who are not within the pale of the church; and answer the ends of their office as much when they do *not* make proselytes as when they do.

If the doctrine of Paley, then, be just, that the sole object of an establishment is religion, it is a strict and legitimate corollary from that doctrine, and a corollary of singular importance, that the object of the establishment is gained just as much when men are rendered religious dissenters, as when they are rendered religious establishment men.

There is however an argument much in the mouths of our adversaries, by which we are sure that this important conclusion will be met. It will be said, that if men should become religious, without being of the church establishment, they would be disposed to destroy the church establishment; the advantage of a church establishment would be lost.

There is a feeling which is by a certain description of churchmen betrayed habitually and in the greatest strength; a feeling, which upon the supposition of a consciousness on their part that church establishments are things not useful, but the contrary, is natural and reasonable; but which, on supposing them persuaded that church establishments are useful, is altogether unaccountable. They are perpetually discovering an inbred apprehension, that if ever men should come to look at establishments impartially, that is, without any prepossession, prejudice, or blind favour, they will be sure not to endure them.

Pray what is the security that men will endure any one factitious establishment, religious or political? There is one sufficient security, which, in the long run, will never fail: that is, the interest of men. Whatever establishments men see it to be for their interest to maintain, they will maintain. It is the apprehension entertained respecting their *utility* that is the security, and the only permanent security, for every human institution. Now, whatever proposed institutions really are useful will sooner or later be found out to be so; and if they are existing institutions, they will seldom run any chance of not being regarded as useful. Is religion, then, useful to man? Are establishments necessary to religion? Upon the answer to these two questions undoubtedly depends the security of establishments. If establishments are favourable to the interests of mankind, they may be shown to be so; and if they are seen to be so, men will uphold them, whether they worship God according to the church forms, or according to forms of their own. According to the only endurable idea of a church establishment, viz. Paley's idea of it, the dissenters are no less interested in the preservation of the establishment than churchmen. It is conducive to that end which churchmen and dissenters have jointly in view; that is, the preservation of religion. Churchmen, therefore, if convinced of the utility of establishments, may be more at their ease. For, if they be useful, it is only necessary to make people see that they are useful, and their permanency is secure; it has in that case the best security which human affairs admit of.

The church establishment, then, as far as it is grounded on utility (on which ground alone, according to Paley, it is entitled to any authority), has nothing whatsoever to fear from the education of the poor in the Lancasterian schools.

There is something exceedingly wayward in the conduct of the intolerant. They disdain this argument. They are perpetually preaching up the great danger which arises from the multiplication of dissenters: they harangue upon the importance of attaching the people as universally as possible to the church. This is one part of their conduct which deserves to be well noted. Again, they proclaim that the institution of a set of dissenting (as they unjustly call the Lancasterian) schools is an institution for gaining over to the dissenters all the people belonging to the church. If this be true, the correspondent proposition is also true; viz. that the institution of a set of Church of England schools would have been an infallible method for gaining over the whole of the dissenters to the Church of England. It is very remarkable that they should so long have been complaining, and so bitterly, of the growth of dissenters; should all this time have been in possession of an infallible secret for extirpating dissenters, viz. providing schools in which on more favourable terms than any where else, the children of dissenters might be educated; and yet should have done so little towards providing those schools. Where language and conduct are so totally at variance, what is to be thought of the conduct,—what of the language?

Having thus seen what is the nature of the principles, or of the theoretical grounds on which reverend and other gentlemen bottom themselves in their opposition to the Lancasterian schools for the poor, we have next to consider, what will not employ us long, the practical deductions to which they proceed.

The more moderate of them, with whom alone we think proper to deal, (satisfied that the others best refute themselves,) do not say that the Lancasterian schools should be suppressed. No; they would permit them for the children of the dissenting poor. All they demand is, —that none of the children of the church should be educated in them.

They mean, therefore, one of two things. They mean, either that the children of the Church of England poor should go without schooling; or that the clergy will provide Church of England schools for them. As the latter is the most favourable supposition, it is that which, for the present, we shall consider.

The clergy, say they, will provide schools for the

poor. What reason have we to believe they *will* do so? Their words. What reason have we to believe they will *not* do so? Their actions.

Should they not provide them, and yet, under the pretence of providing, should succeed in dissuading persons from giving that support to the Lancasterian schools which is necessary for their establishment, what must be the consequence? That the poor must still remain without schooling; though, but for the efforts made to oppose them, schools might so easily have been provided for all.

The clergy, it will be said, are now providing schools; why should it be supposed they will not go on providing them?

What is the cause that the clergy are now providing schools? Joseph Lancaster is the cause. Will any body deny that?

Take away the cause, the effect follows. Will any body deny that? Put an end to the Lancasterian exertions, and to a certainty you put an end likewise to the clerical ones; if any faith is to be put in the most established criterions of human conduct.

If any body is in earnest then to have Church of England schools provided for the children of Church of England poor, he will, if a wise man, zealously support the Lancasterian plans. The success of the Lancasterian plans has roused the clergy to a little exertion; if the Lancasterian plans go on, the continuance of the cause will no doubt produce the continuance of the effect. If the Lancasterian plans should fail for want of encouragement, the exertion which was only roused by these plans would be extinguished along with them.

If there be any sincerity in the present profession of zeal for the education of the poor, it is easy to give a proof of that sincerity which will be altogether indisputable. The clergy have influence and power, and that in large measure. In a popular cause, like this, their power would be irresistible. Let them unite, and let them come forward to parliament with a well considered scheme for affording schooling to the children of all the poor; let the measure be supported with all the power and influence which it is well known they can exert; let them do what it is known they are capable of doing to interest the nation in the scheme; and then we will give them credit for being friends to the education of the poor, though enemies to the schemes of Lancaster.

But if we see them exerting themselves to defeat one practicable and glorious scheme for the education of *all* the poor; while that which they *are* doing in favour of that education, compared with what they *might* do, is so trifling as to deserve no other name than that of a *sham*, they will pardon those of us who are not simpletons, and are a little hackneyed in the ways of men, if we have our own thoughts.

All those men then, of every denomination, throughout the country, who look upon the schooling of the poor as a great good; a good which ought not to be allowed to be defeated by the unfounded terrors, real or pretended, of the authors and abettors of the cry, will be led, we think, if they listen to the dictates of the commonest good sense, to the following practical conclusion:—That nothing less than a legislative provision, adequate to the education of the whole poor of the nation, on the best terms, ought to slacken their efforts in support of the Lancasterian schools. Any thing short of this, it is demonstrated, would, if allowed to destroy the Lancasterian schools, only destroy them without substituting any thing effectual or permanent in their stead. No man will pretend to say that the sudden exertions now making are to be depended upon any longer than the cause which has excited them is to be depended upon. The conduct through every age of the sort of persons by whom they are promoted affords undeniable evidence to this purpose. Even in these recent and enlightened times; when the demand for education has become so great, that they were daily losing ground in public estimation by their neglect of it; all that they have been induced to do has not even been enough to save appearances.

Even their creed, which they say it is of such infinite importance that the children should be taught early, where have they taken any measures that they should so be taught? Though the means of doing it were so simple; though the assembling of the children of each parish, at a convenient hour on the Sunday, was so obvious, so easy, and so effectual a measure, what has been done; we say not for accomplishing this great purpose universally, as it ought to have been done; but even for effecting it in here and there an instance?

When however we are reduced to the necessity of supporting a scheme for the education of the poor by the voluntary contributions of the people, another, and, if possible, a still more important point is to be considered. If the exertions of the clergy in favour of that scheme were as much to be trusted to, as they certainly are *not*, there remains a difference on which every thing depends. The Lancasterian plan is practicable, and indeed easy. The plan proposed by its enemies is altogether impracticable.

With the exception of the few great cities, the poor are distributed in moderate sized towns or villages. For each of these towns and its district, and for an union of two, three, or more villages, one school would completely suffice, and for one school the expense is by the Lancasterian methods reduced to such a trifle, that for each such district it is not surely too much to hope that in voluntary contributions it might be found.

But in each such district, it may be supposed that there are four or five different denominations of christians, and in many there are a good deal more. Annex a creed to the teaching of reading and writing, and you render necessary a school for each particular creed. You need four or five schools instead of one. For this it is vain to hope that voluntary funds can be provided. Surely the public will not be deluded by so deceptious a proposal as this; a proposal which, if it is listened to, is well calculated to *prevent* the schooling of the poor, but is essentially incapable of providing for it.

To sum up the whole then—the problem is, 'To teach reading and writing to the poor.' If a legislative provision is made, all difficulties are removed by the hand of power. If legislative provision is not made, then voluntary contribution alone remains. To the teaching then of reading and writing to the poor, we want to add two circumstances; 1st, cheapness; and 2nd, religious creeds. But these two adjuncts cannot both be at the same time attained. If we have the creeds, we cannot have the cheapness. If we have the cheapness, we cannot have the creeds. Now suppose that we keep to the cheapness; in that case we may have the schools. Out of the three desirable things (1st, schools, 2nd, cheapness, 3rd, creeds) we preserve two, losing only the last. Suppose, on the other hand, that we keep to the creeds; in that case, losing the cheapness, we cannot have the schools; and not having the schools, the children, as they are taught nothing, are not even taught their creeds. In this alternative every thing is lost; by giving up cheapness in the first instance, we eventually give up schools; and, giving up schools, we give up creeds. Adopting the first, then, of these plans, two out of the three desirable things are preserved; adopting the latter, all the three are abandoned. This latter is the alternative embraced by the pretended friends of the church and the poor. All those who embrace the other are, even by consistency, as well as by all other motives, called upon to support the Lancasterian schools.

Having dwelt thus long upon the objections in general which are waged against the schooling plans of the Lancasterians, we shall now proceed to look into what is said against them by some of the most conspicuous of their enemies in particular. We shall begin with Dr Herbert Marsh, who has both preached and published against them a Sermon thus entitled:

'The national Religion the Foundation of national Education. A Sermon preached in the Cathedral Church of St Paul, London, on Thursday, June 13, 1811: being the Time of the yearly Meeting of the Children educated in the Charity-schools in and about the Cities of London and Westminster. To which is added a Collection of Notes, containing Proofs and Illustrations. By Herbert Marsh, D.D. F.R.S. Margaret Professor of Divinity in the University of Cambridge. Preached and printed at the Request of the Society for promoting Christian Knowledge. '*ἱερα τα πατρια τιμησω*.'

'*Ἱερα τα πατρια τιμησω*. 'I will honour the sacred things of my country;' as Dr Marsh would render it, 'I will stick to the Church of England.'—There is something in the use of this motto, on the present occasion, which no right-minded person, we are sure, will overlook. The declaration quoted was made by a heathen; it was a protestation of adherence to the Twelve Gods of Olympus. Quoted, without limitation, as a model and example, by Dr Marsh, it by natural construction implies that the heathen was very right; and that when St Paul preached at Athens other *ἱερα* which were not *τα πατρια*, those of the Athenians who derided him did exactly what they ought to do; those who joined with him acted as badly as the Church of England men who now become Lancasterians. If not; then the adjunct *πατρια* belonging to *ἱερα* is far from being an independent foundation for any particle of respect or attachment; for it is only in so far as the *ἱερα τα πατρια* are *good ἱερα* that it is not every body's duty to *renounce* them. It may be very convenient doctrine for some people to preach, whether openly or by insinuation, that whatever religion is established it is the duty of every man to adhere to it, but we are very sure that no sincere and intelligent Christian, whether of the Church of England or any other *fallible* church, will ever do otherwise than detest such a doctrine.

Another thing which deserves here to be strongly noticed and reprobated is the restrictive and invidious and inadmissible use of the word *πατρια*. *Christianity* is the 'sacred thing' of our country. Who will permit Dr Marsh to tell us that it is only the Church of England? that is, to tell us that the Church of England alone is Christianity! Because the Church of England is the establishment, to call *that* exclusively 'the sacred thing' of the country, as if there were no sacredness in any of the other modifications of religion in the country, authorized and protected by law, is a species of ecclesiastical arrogance, whose day is, happily for the good of mankind, for ever gone by.

Dr Marsh's text is—'Train up a child in the way he should go: and when he is old he will not depart from it.' This, it is evident, is exactly what the Lancasterians propose to do, viz. where it has been hitherto left entirely undone.

Dr Marsh's sermon begins;—'When our religious Reformers had introduced the system of doctrine and discipline which is now established in this kingdom, their next endeavour was to perpetuate that system by an education adapted to it; by training up the children in the way they should go, that, when they were old, they might not depart from it.' This is as extraordinary an assertion, we think, as any that is to be met with in all the pages of ecclesiastical controversy. Who would not suppose, from reading this sentence, that there was attached to our ecclesiastical establishment a system of education, such for example as in the parochial schools of Scotland, for the great body of the people? Whereas, the fact is, that for the education of the great body of the people, no provision is made whatsoever!—But it may be asked, what possible advantage could Dr Marsh propose to himself by this assertion, if it was nothing but a broad negation of notorious fact? Answer, Much. For, if there was any thing at all, how inadequate soever, howsoever totally unworthy of the name of education, either done or only bidden to be done by the church, it would serve as a shift to say, on occasion, that this was all the Doctor meant: while to the great mass of readers the words would in general convey the whole of their natural meaning; that is, they would suggest that the church really has a system of education; and a system established by the Reformers; the reverence of whose name would sanctify the plan on which they had worked. Such is the skill of Dr Marsh, in controversy!

All that he is able to point out (when it is necessary to come to particulars) are those recommendations to learn the elementary points of religion, which all religious communities address to their members. But that a recommendation to godfathers and godmothers, to teach children religion, and to carry them to the bishop to be confirmed, after they can repeat the creed, the Lord's prayer, and the ten commandments, and have been instructed in the church catechism; than which bare *recommendation* to *which persons* certainly never less was done for the religious instruction of its members by any religious community; that *this* should be called education, is surely as extraordinary a use of the word education, as ever was made of that word, or of any other word since the use of speech. If this recommendation, which is all that is performed by the church, were of as much efficacy as by notorious experience it is the reverse and ever must be, it is not reading and writing; therefore it supersedes not what is done by Lancaster; rather, if godfathers and godmothers do what Dr Marsh's word 'education' supposes they do, and what the church takes it for granted they do, it leaves nothing, in the way of teaching *religion*, to be done in the schools for reading and writing; as there is an education, independent of all others, 'adapted to the church system by our religious Reformers,' which has either performed or will perform the business of 'teaching to repeat the creed, the Lord's prayer, the ten commandments, and of instructing in the catechism;' which in fact does all that the church deems necessary as instruction in *religion*, whether the children go to school, or riot in the streets. This passage of Dr Marsh's sermon, then, either implies that the church system of education is efficacious; or that it is not efficacious. If it is efficacious, then is that done by others, which they blame the Lancasterian schools for not doing; if it is not efficacious, then Dr Marsh says there is a system of education attached to the establishment, when, by his own confession, there is no such thing.

A most important passage follows. After telling us what godfathers and godmothers are enjoined to do, Dr Marsh, in his account of the church system of education, says—'In the rubrics annexed to the liturgy, the curate of every parish is enjoined to instruct and examine openly in the church, on Sundays and holidays, so many children of his parish, sent unto him, as he shall think convenient, in some parts of the church catechism. Parents are enjoined to send their children, and masters even their servants and apprentices (if they have not learnt their catechism) obediently to hear and be ordered by the curate, until such time as they have learnt all that is here appointed for them to learn.' (p. 4.) *This*, it is observable, is exactly the plan, which we recommended in a preceding page, for the clergy to pursue, in securing due instruction in the tenets of the church. This is a most excellent plan; and would completely remove all difficulties at once. To this plan, the learning to read and write in the schools of Lancaster surely offers no obstruction. And if the children were all carefully taught their religion every Sunday and holiday by the curate of the parish, they might be taught reading and writing during other days, wherever they could most advantageously receive that teaching. The apprentices here spoken of are exactly on the same footing as the apprentices (for the word *literally* means 'learners') of reading and writing, in the reading and writing shops of reading and writing masters: that is to say, they are young people learning certain mechanical faculties useful for the business of life; and which learning they receive distinctly and separately from that of the principles of religion. Learning these mechanical faculties by which they are to earn their bread is part of their education, and a still more important part than even reading and writing: the young people too *bound* apprentices to the masters of the common trades are far more in the power of those masters, than the *unbound* apprentices in the schools for reading and writing. Yet the legislature in the statutes of apprenticeship never thought of ordaining that only Church of England masters should have Church of England apprentices; or supposed there was any danger in leaving religion to be taught *separately* from mechanical arts. The important question, then, presents itself; whether the clergy actually do what, not only the very nature of their function and belief declares to be their duty, without any particular precept; but what we see is also by an express precept particularly enjoined them; viz. whether they teach the principles of their religion to the *children* of their parishioners on Sundays and holidays? The answer is, That they do so *not at all*! that they entirely omit, neglect, and abandon it! that it is a thing to a great degree even unheard of!—What then are the astonishing facts of this case?—That a great, essential duty of one set of men, obligatory upon them by the very nature of their professed faith, and enjoined them by express command in their standards, is by them entirely betrayed and abandoned; while an accusation is raised for not doing this very duty against other men, whose only object and profession is to teach reading and writing, with which creeds cannot without complete obstruction be, as we have shown, associated. And what is, if possible, still more extraordinary, Dr Marsh brings forward this violated obligation, this neglected duty, this teaching which *ought* to be performed but is *not*, as he well knows; and gives it to operate as a reason against teaching to read and write on the only plan on which, supported only by voluntary, that is if efficient the best resources, it is practicable. What is this but saying, that if one set of men neglect one good thing which they ought to do; another set of men ought to be prohibited from doing another good thing which is altogether independent of the former? That is to say, that one evil, when it happens, should be employed as a reason to make itself be attended with as many other evils as possible!

All inordinate bustle then in the erection of schools as a safeguard to the creed of the church may be spared. If the church only do what she ought all along to have done, her creed will be taught in the very best and most effectual method of teaching it. The bishops, by their sole authority, certainly can without more ado compel all the parochial clergy to perform what the rubrics command them to perform. By this expedient they can make sure immediately of *all* the children belonging to the church being taught their religion. By the slow and partial erection of schools of reading and writing, they cannot immediately, nor to all probability ever, make sure of teaching more than a part. If, then, they shall be seen abandoning that which is *more* effectual for the teaching of religion, adhering to that which is *less*;—abandoning that which they are *commanded* to do, pursuing that which they are *not* commanded to do; it will be plain that neither the interests of religion nor the statutes of the church are the prevailing motive. If they are seen also, in the very same course, opposing a plan for teaching reading and writing, obviously and undeniably *better* adapted for the diffusion of the acquirements of reading and writing, eagerly promoting another, obviously and undeniably *worse* adapted for that diffusion; then it is obvious, that except *opposition* to that diffusion, there is no other motive which can be pointed out. Their conduct, in that case, will be analogous to that of those who say, 'If we cannot get of a good thing all that we wish, let us get all that we can. If we cannot altogether prevent the teaching of reading and writing, let us prevent of it as much as we are able. If it will not do for us to attempt any thing against it by open enmity, let us see what we can accomplish by professed friendship.'

The next paragraph of Dr Marsh is remarkable on another account. He says, (p. 4,) 'From this short statement it appears, that our Reformers themselves laid at least the foundation of a system of religious education, to be conducted under the superintendence of the parochial clergy. And to afford additional security, that this religious education be conducted according to the doctrines of the Church of England, it was enacted by the seventy-seventh canon, that every schoolmaster should not only be licensed by the bishop of the diocese, but *previously subscribe to the liturgy and articles*. And this canon was confirmed by the Act of Uniformity, which requires *every schoolmaster* both to obtain a licence from the bishop, and to declare *that he will conform to the liturgy of the Church of England*, as now by law established. Lastly, by the seventy-ninth canon, all schoolmasters are enjoined, *not only to use the catechism*, but *to bring their scholars to their parish church*.'—We hope all the world will take notice of what we have here. In an enumeration of particulars, for which as a whole the church is held up as an object of admiration and praise, comes, without one single hint of disapprobation, this article! Now what is its strict and direct import? That every dissenter who opens a school ought to be interdicted! that every child who enters a school ought to be taught the Church of England creed, and no other! that schooling absolutely and totally ought to be prohibited to dissenters! And this most flagitious mode of persecution is brought forward as one among the precious reasons for opposing the spread of the Lancasterian schools. As there still are so many persons who betray thoughts which often tread on the very borders of the most odious persecution; and as, *but* for the spirit of the age, such persecution would be, as it has heretofore been seen to be, for the interest of some, it is fortunate that the spirit of the age withholds them from preaching persecution in its most open and most terrific forms.

Dr Marsh's argument is summed up in the following smart syllogistic form:—'The religion *by law established* must always be regarded as the *national* religion. But in every country the national education must be conducted on the principles of the *national religion.* For a violation of this rule would involve, not only an absurdity, but a principle of self-destruction: it would *counteract* by authority what it *enjoins* by authority. No education, therefore, in this country can be entitled to the appellation of *national* where the liturgy is discarded, or where the children attend not the service of the established church.'—(p. 5.)

This argument, notwithstanding its imposing syllogistic appearance, is very lame, even on syllogistic principles. Its syllogistic perfection or imperfection, however, we shall leave to those who have more leisure for the inquiry. Its agreement or non-agreement with matter of fact, and with the good of human kind, is all that we shall examine.

Now, whatever may become of the argument, it is still possible for the Lancasterian schooling to be a thing very good for the people of this country, or very bad. The question of *utility*, then, the only question which any good and wise man will ever think worth considering in the case, is altogether independent of the pompous argument of Dr Marsh. The argument is completely extraneous to it. We may then judge if it ought to have any practical efficacy.

We may observe, in the next place, that it merely turns upon words. It really professes to do nothing more than to determine a controversy of sounds; whether this thing or that thing should be known by this sound or that sound. In truth, it is a mere bit of logomachy.

There are, however, certain perversions of language performed by it, which, as usual, are calculated to mislead and deceive; and to produce, in consequence, mischievous courses of action.

We have seen above, that on all rational principles of nomenclature, *Christianity*, as that alone in its broadest and most liberal acceptation is the religion of this nation, so ought alone to be called the *national* religion. For any of the particular sections into which the Christians of this country are divided to arrogate to their party the name of *national*, when they are *not* the nation, when they are only a *part* of the nation, is the mere rapacity of selfishness, and the overweening of imagined power. That one of these sections is the largest, and is in some respects more favoured than the rest, (which is all that their phrase 'by law established' is permitted to mean,) is far too narrow a foundation on which to claim the epithet of *national;* unless the rapacity of selfishness be that which should determine. In places where only *one* form of Christianity is permitted, *there* to be sure that *one* form may, without absurdity, be denominated the *national* religion. The Cortes of Spain, who have ordained the Catholic religion to be the *exclusive* religion of Spaniards, may with propriety pronounce the Catholic religion the *national* religion of Spain. But in England, where (thank God) Christianity in *all* its forms* is authorized and protected by law, (i.e. in the most essential import 'established by law,') for *Church-of-Englandism* to arrogate to itself the name of *national*, is only to grasp at as much of that *exclusive* practice which distinguishes Spain; that is, as much of persecution; as the spirit of the nation will bear. If it be said that this is only the persecution of a name; be it remembered, that the power of affixing names of one sort to one party, and of another sort to another party, may often be no *trifling* power of persecution; and also, that it is a power of persecution which may very often be capable of exercise, when the time for exercising any other has passed by.

Again; if you are permitted to attach any *name* to any party, and then by that name, as a link, to attach to the party any thing else you please, it is pretty plain what important effects you may produce by names. Thus, for example: attach the word *national* to the church, and then go on, giving it every thing else it chooses to call national; first, the *national* education; next, if you

* Unless in as far as the penal laws against Catholics still form an unhappy exception; or the persecution which still hangs over the head of Unitarianism.

please, the *national* wealth; and the *national* understanding; and the *national* virtue: you may thus prove that no man ought to have education, wealth, understanding, or virtue, but a Church of England man; or at any rate that his education, wealth, understanding, or virtue, ought not to be called *national*, nor held as any *part* of the *national* education, wealth, understanding, or virtue. On these clerical principles of logic, it is evident that the calling of names is no trifle. *Hæ nugæ in seria ducunt mala.*

The *national education*, says Dr Marsh. By this phrase, any man who had not a particular purpose to serve, would mean *the education of the nation*, that is, of the individuals of whom the nation is composed. 'But,' says Dr Marsh, 'in every country the national education must be conducted on the principles of the national religion.' He does not mean that the individuals of whom the nation is composed should all be educated on the principles of the church called the Church of England, but each on the principles of his own church; that is, that the national education should be conducted on the broad basis of Christianity; in which the Lancasterians entirely agree with him. According then to the only rational and proper meaning of the term *national education*, Dr Marsh himself allows that it ought to be carried on upon no other principle than that which is adopted by the Lancasterians.

Dr Marsh says, 'A violation of this rule would involve not only an absurdity, but a principle of self-destruction.' That the violation of a rule, if it is a good rule, should involve a principle of self-destruction, is the very thing which is the most to be desired; as it thus necessarily works its own remedy. Dr Marsh proceeds to tell us *how* 'a violation of this rule' would involve all this: 'It would counteract by authority what it enjoins by authority.' What the violation of a rule *counteracts* is plain enough; it is the rule. Now observe, that what the violation of Dr Marsh's rule *counteracts*, it also *enjoins;* that is to say, *the violation* of a rule *enjoins* the rule! This is only worth observing, as it proves, either that Dr Marsh knows not when he expresses himself unintelligently; or that his cause will not bear to be spoken of in clear and consistent terms.

Authority counteracting what *authority* enjoins, is no such rare thing either in church or state, that Dr Marsh should affect to be so unacquainted with it. And when it happens, the counteraction will almost always be found to be a *good* thing, the injunction a *bad.* How many persecuting laws, for example, still remain in the statute book, which are not enforced by the courts of law?

The education then proposed by the clergy is so far from being *national* that it is distinctively meant to be confined to a particular *part* of the nation; and is by its very conditions *exclusive* of a great proportion of the nation. The term *national* cannot therefore be applied to it without the most violent abuse of language. The Lancasterian plans, on the other hand, are calculated entirely and purposely to embrace the nation; and, if they are but properly supported, will exhibit *a national education* in the truest and happiest sense of the term; in the only sense in which the Lancasterians have ever used the term, or in which they can have any wish to use it.

Dr Marsh asks; 'Do we act consistently, if, while we *profess* to believe all the articles of the Christian faith, we encourage a system of education from which those articles of faith are *excluded*?' (p. 7.) Let the use here made of the word *excluded* be well attended to. To teach the children of the poor to read their Bibles, without saying one word against the articles of the Church of England faith, is to *exclude* the articles of that faith! The BIBLE *exclude* the articles of the Church of England faith!

Teaching to read and write is one part of education. Teaching apprentices the different trades and professions is another and a still greater branch of education. To this last no creed is attached. Do the clergy 'act consistently' who have no objection to the *exclusion*, as Dr Marsh calls it, of their creed from one 'system' (by which he can only mean *branch*) 'of education,' when they are desirous to stir heaven and earth on account of its (so called) exclusion from another, to which it is still less capable of being attached?

Yes, yes; the clergy would act a very consistent part, and, what is still better than even a consistent part, they would act a *good* part, a part highly conducive to the well-being of their countrymen, if they were to encourage, for the teaching of reading and writing, that system, whatever it may be, which is most happily adapted to that particular purpose; they themselves teaching, as they are commanded to teach, religion and the articles of their faith to the children of their own church, separately from other branches of education, (from the apprenticement of reading and writing, as from that of any other mechanical art,) on the Sundays and holidays.

The use here made of the term 'Christian faith', too, is by no means unworthy of notice. It is made to mean, and to mean *exclusively*, (for the articles here spoken of are *exclusively* the articles of that church) 'the faith of the Church of England.' The consequence is, (only Dr

Marsh leaves it to be drawn by others,) that no faith but the Church of England faith is *Christian* faith. Allow the politico-theologians all they choose to assume, and all that would hence be *consistent* for them (as they call it) to do, and we should have a fine world!

Dr Marsh continues: 'Can the clergy especially, who not only *subscribe* to the liturgy and articles, but even hold their preferments by this *very tenure*, conscientiously support any other than a *Church of England* education? Can they do it without *betraying* the cause which they are pledged to *defend*?' (p. 7.) By *Church of England education*, we should suppose, must be meant *instruction in the doctrines and discipline of the Church of England*. Now, sure we are, that the clergy may very conscientiously support the best scheme for teaching to read and write, (which no more opposes the Church of England education than teaching to weave and to sew,) while they themselves give, as they are in duty bound, and as they are commanded to give, the religious branch of instruction to the children of their respective flocks.

But suppose the case were not so completely stript of all difficulty as it is; suppose, in this case, as in most other cases, a portion of one sort of good were to be given up, for the sake of obtaining a portion (still greater in value) of some other sort of good. Suppose the church to be the circumstance affected; that by giving up a small portion of good relative to the church, and by that alone, a portion of good, clearly and undeniably outweighing that good, were to some other purpose to be obtained; we put it to Dr Marsh, and to all who resemble Dr Marsh, whether the most conscientious clergyman would not of the two goods make choice of the greater, even though it were the church that was to be the sufferer; whether conscience (if by that be meant a well founded sense of duty) would not even compel him to make that choice? Now, as it does clearly appear, that to attach creeds to the teaching of reading and writing must render that teaching so expensive as to be unobtainable by the only methods as yet proposed, might not the most conscientious clergyman consider that teaching to be so great a good, that (even if it were not altogether free from danger to the church to disjoin the religious branch of education from that as from various other branches) he must yet regard it as his duty to recommend that disjunction; to recommend it as what, after its advantages and disadvantages were weighed, he believed to be best for mankind upon the whole?—How much stronger is this conclusion, when it is shown that there is no danger to the church at all!

The next sentence, in this passage of Dr Marsh, is remarkable on another account. After the preceding questions relative to the people and clergy of the church, he says, with regard to all *Dissenters* holding any test-demanding office, 'It may indeed be asked, whether *every* man, from the lowest to the highest, who holds an office of trust or power, whether religious or civil, which he could not have obtained but by *professing himself a member of the National Church*, is not bound by such profession, if not openly to discountenance, at least not openly to promote, a system of education from which the national religion is *discarded*.' (p. 8.) Take notice here, in passing, of the use of the word *discarded*. The BIBLE, (being taught) *discards* the Church of England religion!—Is the binding a son an apprentice without inserting an article for the teaching of religion ever called *discarding* religion?—We see to what uses language serves, in the hands of such a man as Dr Marsh*.' All this, however, is by the bye; what we have at present in view is Dr Marsh's construction of the Test Act.[25] He gives us another passage on that head. '*Every* man who accepts an office of trust or power even in the civil administration, is by law required *to profess himself a member of their church*, by assisting at the most solemn of its rites, the celebration of the Lord's supper.' (p. 28.) We here see what, in the opinion of Dr Marsh, is the situation of the Dissenters. It is neither more nor less than that they are absolutely excluded from offices of power and trust. If they take the test, they by that act declare themselves Church of England men. If they do not take the test, and yet hold offices of power and trust, as by the acts of indemnity they are enabled to do, they yet, by the very act of 'holding the office,' says Dr Marsh, 'profess themselves members of the national church;' that is to say, they are guilty of an act of solemn and legally-operative falsehood; or, in other words, they are guilty of an act which is tantamount to perjury!—All that we desire to say upon this is—Can it be wise, right, reasonable, fitting, or tolerable, that such a test as this should exist? The PHILANTHROPIST has in this same number (p. 17 to 22) made some observations on the effects of the test laws, to which we here beg the reader to turn back: it is a subject which deserves that he should take so much trouble about it. Let us hear also what Dr Paley (which is authority) says to the point:—'It has indeed been asserted,' says that celebrated theologian, 'that discordancy of religions, even supposing each religion to be

* The education among the blackguards in the streets (for that too is education, though of a bad sort,) did any body ever hear Dr Marsh complaining that the *National Religion* was discarded from *that*? It is not discarded by a *mischievous* education, then; it is only discarded by a *good* one.

free from any errors that affect the safety or the conduct of government, is enough to render men unfit to act together in public stations. But upon what argument, or upon what experience, is this assertion founded? I perceive no reason why men of different religious persuasions may not sit upon the same bench, deliberate in the same council, or fight in the same ranks, as well as men of various or opposite opinions upon any controverted topic of natural philosophy, history, or ethics*.'—Surely, too, if men of different religious opinions may thus act together, they may be taught reading and writing together.

We now come to show that there is no doctrine, how explicitly soever renounced and reprobated by the greatest men whom the church has produced, how completely soever proved to be mischievous in all its effects both religious and political, which Dr Marsh and his fellows are not prepared to bring forward in glittering array against the Lancasterians. The reader will recollect what we quoted above from Dr Paley respecting the unavoidable corruption and debasement of religion which springs from the *alliance* (as it is called) of the church with the state. He will recollect also, we hope, what we proved respecting the *political* use of such an alliance; that it never could be any thing else than the protection of misrule: and the obvious conclusion which thence resulted, viz. that the alliance of church and state is, to the last mite, the union of religious abuse and corruption with political abuse and corruption. If he does not recollect all this distinctly, and the grounds on which it proceeded, we beg he will turn back and read carefully the 141st and four succeeding pages. He may

* Paley's Principles of Moral and Political Philosophy, b. vi. ch. 10. vol. ii. p. 338.

then make his own commentary on the following passage which we quote from Dr Marsh.

'We are now concerned with the *facts*, that there *is* a religion by law established in this country; that the State *has* made an alliance with the Church; that it has allied itself with the *Church of England*; that for the security of this church provision has been made, not only by repeated acts of parliament, but by His Majesty's coronation oath; and lastly, that *every* man who accepts an office of trust or power, even in the *civil* administration, is by law required to profess himself *a member of this church* by assisting at the most solemn of its rites, the celebration of the Lord's supper. Now whether men consider religion as *merely* an engine of the state, or regard it also, as they ought, for its own excellence and truth, as the means of obtaining happiness in *another world*, they must in either case admit that its *alliance* with the state implies *utility* to the state. Without a prospect of some *advantage* to be derived from the church, the state would have neither sought its alliance, nor granted it protection. Whether our ancestors judged *rightly* in this respect, or whether civil society (as some modern theorists imagine) can be as *well* conducted *without* the aid of an established religion, yet, as long as the present constitution remains, it is both the duty and the interest of *all* who are members of it to adhere to the principles on which it is founded. It is the interest of *statesmen*, as well as of *clergymen*, to preserve to *each* of the contracting parties sufficient power to enable it to fulfil the *terms* of the compact; to enable therefore the church to render that service to the state which the state requires, and compensates by reciprocal aid. By weakening *either* of the contracting parties we diminish the strength of the *whole*. By detaching men from the *church* we create divisions in the *state* which may end with the dissolution of *both*. So congenial is the *Church* of England with the *State* of England, that, since their alliance at the Reformation, they have neither *fallen* alone nor *risen* alone. They *fell* together in the reign of the first Charles; they *rose* together in the reign of the second Charles. Let not statesmen therefore imagine that the church may fall without danger to *themselves*. If no reverence, no devotion is excited by the *divine origin* of our religion, yet, unless men reject also the opinion that religion advances the good of *civil society*, they will pause at least, before they contribute to the dissolution of an alliance which has so long and so usefully subsisted. They will be cautious how they treat the institutions of the church as unnecessary ingredients in a plan of national education. They will be cautious how they patronize seminaries from which the doctrine and discipline of the Church of England are openly and avowedly discarded. But if such patronage is bestowed, where we have most reason to expect support to the establishment, we may then despair of being able to fulfil the *condition* of our alliance. Our *utility* will cease. We shall lose the *power* of doing good. No residence, no preaching, no catechizing will further avail. Our flocks will have deserted us; they will have grown wiser than their guides; and the *national* creed will have become too narrow for minds accustomed to the liberal basis.'

We add nothing at all to this. It is far too luminous to need any lights thrown upon it extraneously.

We shall conclude this part of the discussion with an argument which we really should hope, notwithstanding the sneers of Dr Marsh against *liberality*, would have an effect, and that an important one, upon all the liberal part even of the Church of England; upon all those who join not with Dr Marsh in his contempt of liberality. It has been proved, and indeed is so obvious and certain as not to stand in need of any proof, that by enlarging the basis on which schools are erected, so as to admit into them persons of all religious persuasions, education can be much more easily and completely diffused, than on the exclusionary and confined basis of particular and distinctive creeds. This extension consists in embracing in the scheme of instruction only so much of religious doctrine as all Christians are agreed in. Oh, but, cry the antagonists, this is to give up religion; or at any rate the religion of the Church of England. Now it is remarkable, and we trust it will make the impression which it ought to make, that Dr Paley, the admired Dr Paley, the grand defender of Christianity, the greatest ornament of the last age of the church, recommends this very same expedient; this abstracting from all the disputed and distinctive parts of religion, not for schools of reading and writing merely, but for the very religious service of the church. 'We allow,' says he, 'to each church the truth of its peculiar tenets, and all the importance which zeal can ascribe to them. We dispute not here the right or the expediency of framing creeds, or of imposing subscriptions. But why should every position which a church maintains be woven with so much industry into her forms of public worship? Some are offended, and some are excluded: this is an evil in itself, at least to *them:* and what advantage or satisfaction can be derived to the *rest*, from the separation of their brethren, it is difficult to imagine; unless it were a duty, to publish our system of polemic divinity, under the name of making confession of our faith every time we worship God; or a sin, to agree in religious exercises with those from whom we differ in some religious opinions. Indeed, where one man thinks it his duty constantly to worship a Being, whom another cannot, with the assent of his conscience, permit himself to worship at all, there seems to be no place for comprehension, or any expedient left but a quiet secession. All other differences may be compromised by silence. If sects and schisms be an evil, they are as much to be avoided by one side as the other. If sectaries are blamed for taking unnecessary offence, established churches are no less culpable for unnecessarily giving it: they are bound at least to produce a command, or a reason of equivalent utility, for shutting out any from their communion, by mixing with divine worship doctrines, which, whether true or false, are unconnected, in their nature, with devotion*.' But if a scheme for the embracing of all or almost all sects of Christianity in the same religious worship, merely by abstaining from the mention or inculcation of polemical or distinctive points, would be a good measure; surely it must be very wrong to oppose a scheme for embracing all sorts of Christians in one set of schools, for the mere purpose of learning to read and write!

The schools which our adversaries are now making a show of being in earnest to erect, must be either upon the comprehensive principle here recommended by Paley even for religious worship; or they must be upon the exclusive and narrow principle. If they are upon the exclusive principle, every disinterested and intelligent person will presently see, that they are inferior to the Lancasterian schools in the most essential and important of almost all respects: and whoever is in earnest

* Paley's Principles of Moral and Political Philosophy, b. v. ch. 5. vol. ii. p. 66.

about the education of the poor, whether Church of England man or Dissenter, ought still to support the Lancasterian schools. If they are upon the comprehensive principle, then all objection to the Lancasterian principle, which is the same, is given up. Then the Lancasterians and the clergy are concurrent. For we can venture to promise, whether the clergy would or would not permit a Dissenter to be the master of any of their schools, that the Lancasterians would have no objection to making Church of England men masters in theirs. In point of fact they have already done so; and examples could now be pointed out of persons belonging to the Church of England officiating as masters in schools erected by the Lancasterians. Indeed, as often as a Church of England man presented himself for the office of schoolmaster, better qualified than his competitors, the Lancasterians must have a complete and adequate motive to employ him; only restraining him, as they would a Quaker, a Baptist, a Presbyterian, or any other, from teaching so much of his creed as would tend to exclude from his school the children of any man of another persuasion to whom it might be useful to repair to it. On this principle we cannot imagine that the heart of any enlightened man, from one end of the kingdom to another, will not be with them.

There is another Publication which ambitiously exhibits itself in the ranks of our opponents, and has come forward with an elaborate and designing article against the Lancasterians. For this Publication it will be merely sufficient to point out its own inconsistencies. Its various writers are upon this subject evidently not in tune; and the leader of the band is not skilful enough to reduce them to concord. In the last number of the publication called The Quarterly Review,[26] there are two articles on clerical or theological matters: the one, on the Bishop of Lincoln's Refutation of Calvinism; the other, on Bell's and Lancaster's Systems of Education. The very first paragraph of the review on the important subject handled by the Prelate says, 'Few persons can be much conversant in theological controversy, without frequently regretting that discussion should have been started on many subjects decidedly above the grasp of human intellect. The Bible is a plain book, which all may understand with ease. The points of necessary belief there laid down are few and simple, and the path of duty is so straight that none can miss it. Why then have Christians in all ages been so busily employed in tracing theological subtleties, and multiplying creeds and articles of faith? Why have they thought it necessary to stir up abstruse questions which have exasperated many bad passions, and generated many unhappy divisions, while they have been productive of no counterbalancing advantages, and have diverted the attention from solid practical duties to thorny and fruitless speculations? Why, too, have men of the most enlarged and liberal views, and the most exempt from bigotry, added fuel to the flames of controversy; and, by taking part in these discussions, given them a degree of firmness and consistency which they could not have otherwise acquired*?' It is natural to suppose that the person chosen for the discussion of a subject so profoundly theological, of so important a nature, and handled in so new a manner by so elevated and dignified a churchman as the Bishop of Lincoln, would be a man the most profoundly and purely theological belonging to the party from whom the publication in question

* Quarterly Review, October 1811, p. 191.

proceeds; would be a man reckoned far more trustworthy on theological ground, than the man necessary for the sort of half secular, half ecclesiastical subject involved in the Lancasterian controversy, for which any linsey-woolsey, any amphibious brother, who had a pen ready for all purposes, would suffice. We shall consider the above passage, therefore, as containing a specimen of the best considered and most approved theological sentiments of the publication in question. Nor need it be ashamed of them: we see they are concurrent with those we had just quoted from no less an authority than Dr Paley. Dr Paley, then, and the Quarterly Review agree in recommending that precise view of theological creeds and theological controversy, on which, in regard to religion, the Lancasterian schools are founded. 'The Bible,' says the writer in this article, 'is a plain book, which all may understand with ease. The points of necessary belief there laid down are few and simple, and the path of duty is so strait that none can miss it. Why then have Christians in all ages been so busily employed in tracing theological subtleties, and multiplying creeds and articles of faith?' Can words more distinctly imply—a censure of the present proceedings for entangling with creeds the education of the poor—approbation of the proceedings of the Lancasterians? In the Lancasterian schools, the Bible, that 'plain book, which all may understand with ease;' in which 'the points necessary for belief are few and simple,' and 'the path of duty so strait that none can miss it,' is read, and the points of belief and practice which are thus easily discerned, thus incapable of being missed, produce their true and native impressions. A party calling themselves the Church condemn and reprobate this plan, and urge instead of it, that 'tracing of subtleties,' that 'multiplication of creeds and articles of faith,' which the theological writer in the Quarterly Review so strongly condemns; condemns as being productive of many of the worst of evils, while it is attended with '*no* counterbalancing advantage.' Even *liberality*, which Dr Marsh sneers at, is spoken of as being a respectable quality, by this writer; who goes so far as to treat *bigotry* itself in a contemptuous manner. All this is very wonderful, compared with what we have in the same publication on the subject of the Lancasterian schools. There it is said that Dr Marsh 'exposes the specious and insidious argument that no injury is done to the national religion, because Mr Lancaster teaches nothing hostile to it*.' What is recommended, we have seen, by Dr Paley, and the writer of the article on the work of the Bishop of Lincoln, with regard to religious services themselves, is here, when recommended only for schools of reading and writing, denominated 'specious and insidious' by this Lancasterian antagonist. Now, how is it *exposed*, as he says? How is it shown to be specious and insidious? By that which, we trust, we have already sufficiently exposed to the eyes of all sincere and intelligent men; by preaching up that most fraudulent and treacherous of all doctrines, the alliance of church and state. Regardless of what reason so distinctly proclaims respecting the abuse and corruption which it is of the very essence of this alliance to produce both in church and state; regardless even of what such men as Dr Paley have written upon the subject, this writer has not been ashamed to tread over this ground in the very footsteps of Dr Marsh. 'Mr Lancaster,' he says, 'finds that some tenets must be presupposed, and holds it an essential part of education to teach what, according to his creed;

* Quarterly Review, October 1811, p. 289.

are necessary religious opinions.' [This is not correct; but let it pass:—the writer goes on:—] 'We entirely agree with him; but the question thus arises, upon his own grounds, what religious opinions are necessary; and here the well-being of the state must be considered, as well as the moral improvement of the individual.' Oh, it must, must it? The question with this writer is not, what religion is *true*? what religion is most conducive to the 'moral improvement of the individual?' but what religion is most conducive to the well-being of the state. 'Well-being of the state!'—If by that be meant the mere interests of the individuals exercising the powers of government, what is meant is neither more nor less than that the interests of religion should be sacrificed to assist individuals in sacrificing the interests of the community. If by the 'well-being of the state' be meant *good government*, we have already shown, and we think undeniably, that the alliance of religion with government, any further than as its operation on the 'moral improvement of the individual' may be called alliance, is capable of doing nothing but pure mischief. Such is the 'exposure' given by Dr Marsh and the *Quarterly Review* to the 'specious and insidious' doctrine of Dr Paley and the *Quarterly Review*!

'The system of English policy,' continues the Lancasterian Reviewer, 'consists of church and state; they are the two pillars of the temple of our prosperity; they must stand together or fall together.' This is neither more nor less than naked browbeating assertion, founded upon the most erroneous, and not only upon the most erroneous, but the most mischievous of all political doctrines. Who is obliged to believe this Reviewer, that the British constitution is so weak a fabric that it cannot stand unless it has a particular form of a church to support it? For our parts, we do not think of the British constitution so contemptuously. If it had not within *itself* all the pillars necessary for its support, it would be little worthy of the admiration of intelligent men. 'The English system of policy,' he says, 'consists of church and state.' This is a mere vulgar form of speech which means nothing. A system of policy consists of three parts: 1st, A legislative power,—2nd, An executive power,—3rd, A judicative power. Is the church any of these? The ecclesiastical arrangements are neither more nor less than one among the other sets of arrangements which the supreme powers of the state have thought proper to make; and it would be just as wise, and as correct political doctrine, to say the army and the state, or the navy and the state, and that they must stand together or fall together. Indeed, the latter would be nearest the truth; as a military force, more or less, is a necessary adjunct of government, but a particular religious creed not at all. The Reviewer goes on: 'Now to propose a system of national education, of which it is the avowed and distinguishing principle that the children shall not be instructed in the national religion, is to propose what is palpably absurd. This position is irrefragably stated by Dr Herbert Marsh. "*The religion by law established*," he says, "*must always be regarded as the* national *religion. But in every country the national* education *must be conducted on the principles of the national* religion. *For a violation of this rule would involve not only an absurdity, but a principle of self-destruction; it would* counteract *by authority what it* enjoins *by authority**." ' This is passing strange. That sentence of Dr Marsh's sermon, which we have just shown to contain no two coherent ideas; to be a mere

* Quarterly Review, October 1811, p. 289.

tissue of inconsistent terms, involving propositions which no mortal in his senses could entertain, is swallowed with delight by this sapient Reviewer; is adopted by him, and even held out by him to the world, as 'irrefragable statement.' A *violation* of a rule *enjoining* that same rule; a violation of a rule complained of because it involves a principle of self-destruction, that is, *the remedy of its own evil*; this is called 'irrefragable statement' by the Quarterly Reviewer who attacks the Lancasterian schools!

To propose the Lancasterian scheme of education is, we see, called proposing 'an education of which it is the avowed and distinguishing principle that the children shall *not* be instructed in the national religion.' This Reviewer, it is evident, is but little scrupulous about weighing his terms, when the question is to prostrate an adversary. He seems to be well acquainted with the force of the lesson, *fortiter calumniari, semper aliquid hæret*. He speaks in his Review of 'rash and desperate quackery;' he might have spoken, too, of rash and desperate calumny; and have weighed which was the heaviest in mischief. When any thing to be done is spoken of as being 'the avowed and distinguishing principle' of another thing, it is understood that the latter operates directly and primarily to produce the former. Thus, it is the avowed and distinguishing principle of medicine, that disease should not exist; it is the avowed and distinguishing object of law, that injustice should not exist. In the same manner, if it be the avowed and distinguishing object of the Lancasterian plans, that the national religion should not be taught, the Lancasterians must do what in them lies to *prevent* the national religion from being taught; which is not true, in whatsoever unjustifiable and restrictive sense the term *national religion* may be employed. Notwithstanding this unprincipled assertion, it is true, and notoriously true, that the Lancasterian plans do *nothing* to prevent the teaching of the Church of England religion; on the contrary, they do a thing of infinite importance in aid of the teaching of it; they instruct the people to read their bibles. Who would suffer this Reviewer to say that of the whole train of apprenticeships for educating the youth to the knowledge and practice of the different crafts, 'it is the avowed and distinguishing principle that the national religion shall not be taught'? Yet in this respect they stand on the same foundation as the Lancasterian schools for teaching to read and write, even if the Bible itself were not read or heard of in those schools. If the Reviewer should say that he did not mean all that is here imputed to his words; it will not do, to use equivocating expressions that naturally import, and are calculated to suggest, what is injurious and untrue, and then to say that a man did not mean what is supposed; for this is one of the most usual of the fraudulent tricks of those who basely wish to insinuate what they dare not avow.

There is another point of vast importance, which it has been the interest of those who hate our work to keep out of sight in this controversy; and which the length to which we have been carried in answering their arguments does but barely permit us to mention. We shall do it justice on another occasion, if the case should seem to require it.—It is to be remarked, that religious distinctions among the people are an evil. They are a source of division which is at no time without its effects; and of which the effects at certain times, which may always arise, would be of the very worst as well as the most violent kind. These evils are, however, far less than those which would spring from any violent methods to put an end to those distinctions; and therefore they must be borne. But it is the business of a wise system of policy to do whatever may be done to mitigate and temper the dissocial feelings which are apt to spring from those distinctions. It is a fact, that an Establishment is a peculiar cause of those animosities and hatreds. If establishments are attended with other advantages which counter-balance this evil, and notwithstanding this evil render them a good upon the whole,—be it so; this we do not for the present dispute. Still it is true that an establishment counts among its disadvantages that of exasperating the discordant passions which diversity of religion produces. It is well known, even in a private family, that the partiality of the parents to one of the children produces discord and unhappiness in the family: now it is certain, as has been often remarked, that a state is only a family on a great scale. When princes count among their weaknesses a propensity to favouritism, it is well known to what a degree the favourite inflames and animates all the discordant passions which usually inhabit a court. The pride, and jealousy, and persecuting spirit which are found in so many of the clergy of an established church, especially a clergy consisting of ranks, from a rank of great poverty and degradation to a rank of great riches and power, are a peculiar cause of aggravation and excitement to all the bad passions which it is incident to the case to engender. Now the nature of the circumstances sufficiently declares what an enlightened and prudent policy in this case would dictate. That is;—to do whatever could be expediently done to weaken the force of these divisive sentiments or feelings; to avoid every thing (not commanded by preponderating utility of another sort) that had any tendency to add to the force of these sentiments. If unity of *opinions* among a whole people be, as it is, a thing impossible; there is no such impossibility in a general harmony of *affections*; which ought ever to be aimed at, as one of the first of national glories, and of national advantages, by every patriotic government. This being so obviously and certainly the case, our experience and knowledge of human nature loudly proclaim to us, that one of the most efficient of all means for mollifying the discordant feelings apt to arise from religious diversities, and for training the differing classes of religionists in habits of mutual sympathy and benevolence, is the right ordering of the education of the young. It is well known how powerfully it always operates to produce unity and harmony of feeling, to be educated together. This is a principle, a fact in the history of human nature, which an enlightened politician would hold precious. This he would turn to the most important account. In this he would perceive immediately an instrument wherewith to perform, in the best possible way, some of the best possible effects. Most assuredly it would never be his object to educate asunder, in distinct and discordant seminaries, those religious diversities of the people, whose differences of opinion he was desirous should produce as little discordance as possible of *feeling and affection*. This could serve only to give these discordancies of affection and feeling their utmost possible malignity and strength; could only teach the different classes of religionists to hate and contend with one another from their tenderest years. On the other hand, the educating of them together would produce the very contrary effects; would teach them, if they must differ in opinions, as when grown up they certainly would, (for that is incident to human nature,) to *agree* to differ; *i.e.* to have different opinions, without quarrelling with one another, or hating one another, on that account.[27] Of a truly enlightened policy, then, it would most certainly be an object, and one of the most highly respected and dear, that, as far as could possibly be done, the different religious classes of the people should be educated *together*; that is to say, that as much of education as possible, all that consisted not in the teaching of religion, should be taught in seminaries to which the children of all the religious classes should be encouraged to resort indiscriminately; and that no other part of education but that solely and distinctively which consists in teaching religion, should be encouraged to be performed in separate and exclusive places of instruction. To this obvious and important policy,—in the present state of the world important beyond all former example,—the present outcry is directly opposed. That the people in general, or the legislature, will lend themselves to the gratification of sectarian passions in so important a point as this, we are extremely averse to suppose. If they do, sure we are, it will be under the influence of an enormous mistake; and with no little danger of present and eventual mischief to their country.

To us it would appear, that the very statement of the scheme which is set up in opposition to the Lancasterian schools, would be sufficient to avert from it the mind of every thinking and patriotic person. Let us suppose that the support of the nation is withdrawn from the Lancasterian schools, and bestowed upon those who are calling themselves the Church and the Clergy: Suppose the schools to be erected, at public or private expense, and tuition begun; what happens? The children of

Dissenters, forming a large (our opponents say a very large) and growing proportion of the population, present themselves for schooling;—and are excluded. A large proportion, then, of the population are, as far as the scheme of our opponents is concerned, to be deprived of the benefits of education; to have an invidious and exasperating distinction, of a new sort, set up between them and Churchmen! What are the sort of sentiments which are likely to be engendered in the breasts of dissenting parents by a treatment such as this? Suppose that along with the schools from which the Dissenters are excluded, schools are supported by the Dissenters for themselves; are our opponents so blind as not to see that if danger any where, there is much more of it to the Church in this scheme than in that which they oppose? The Dissenters are sure to surpass the Establishment, in zeal, industry, attention, and that skill which is the necessary result of labour and pains. Our opponents are among the foremost to proclaim and to lament this result, in the teaching of religion itself, where the clergy have a more peculiar concern; dwelling, in the most emphatic terms, on the growth of Dissenters; on the proselytizing arts and success of the dissenting clergy; and on the want of equal zeal and industry among the clergy of the Church. They are right in their notion of the cause; and they can hardly fail to see that it is incurable. The men who have every thing depending on their zeal, industry, and success, always have been, and always will be, far more industrious, skilled, and successful, than those who have little or nothing depending on their zeal, industry, and success. The consequences, therefore, to the Church, of the scheme proposed by her present professing votaries, would be,—not that all the children of Churchmen would be educated in the church schools; but that a large proportion, seeing the children of Dissenters better educated, would go to the dissenting schools, where it is proposed by the clergy that dissenting creeds should be taught.—What the Church, therefore, would gain in respect to *this proportion* of the poor, would be, that instead of being educated in Lancasterian schools without any change of creed, they would be educated in the dissenting schools with a total change of creed. In respect to *the other proportion* who might continue to be educated in the schools of the Church, they would be worse educated than those in the schools of the Dissenters. The mass of the population would thus be formed into two remarkable divisions: 1. that of those educated in Church schools, worse educated; 2. that of those educated in Dissenting schools, better educated.—Is this a state of affairs that could fail to be detrimental to the Church? Would it not be better for her to see her proportion of the population as well educated as others, in schools in which, without distinction of creeds, persons of all religious denominations were admitted on equal terms?

NOTES

Essay on Education

1. p. 48, **Hartley.** David Hartley (1705–57), physician and philosopher. He published *Observations on Man, his Frame, Duty and Expectations* in 1749 and developed a theory of association of ideas with a physiological basis of 'vibrations' in the 'medullary substance' of the brain. Mill wrote to Place: 'Hartley is a book well worth your having . . . The doctrine of vibrations is altogether gratuitous. But I think I shall one day be able to make it appear that the account he renders of the world of ideas is the true one. He himself is an obscure and very dull writer . . . but his doctrine might be put in a point of view so clear and striking, that metaphysics thereafter would not be very mysterious.' (B.M. Addn. MSS 35,152. Mill to Place, 6 September, 1815.)

2. p. 48, **Condillac.** Etienne de Condillac (1750–80). His major work, *Traité des Sensations* (1754), derived all mental phenomena from sense-experience.

3. p. 48, **Dr Reid.** Dr Thomas Reid (1710–92). Professor of Moral Philosophy at Aberdeen 1751, and Glasgow 1764. He published *Inquiry into the Human Mind* in 1764 and his most important doctrine was that we apprehended the external world by a process of immediate intuition: he was thus a critic of the English empirical tradition of Locke, Berkeley and Hume, who held that the mind was the passive receiver of sensations. Among Reid's followers was Dugald Stewart, under whom Mill studied at Edinburgh and for whom he retained a lasting respect, despite their philosophical differences.

4. p. 48, **Kant.** Immanuel Kant (1724–1804), eminent German philosopher of Königsberg, whose theories were diametrically opposed to those of Mill. Kant held that sense-experience itself meant nothing until the organising and reasoning

powers of the mind resolved it into what we call knowledge. Thus he attached an importance to the reasoning powers of the mind which Mill denied, and unlike Mill was not an environmentalist. His *Critique of Pure Reason* appeared in 1781.

5. p. 52, **Mr Hobbs.** Thomas Hobbes (1588–1679), English political philosopher and author of *Leviathan.* Perhaps more important than his associationist theories is his firm belief in hedonism.

6. p. 54, **Mr Locke.** John Locke (1632–1704), English philosopher. His principal work in philosophy is the *Essay Concerning Human Understanding*, from which this passage is quoted. Mill described it as 'a sort of fundamental book'. Locke is an important contributor to the English empirical tradition which Mill largely followed.

7. p. 55, **Mr Hume.** David Hume (1711–76). Scottish philosopher, perhaps the ablest of the empiricists. His moral and economic theories are also in the utilitarian tradition.

8. p. 66, **'Speculations . . . may be divided into two great classes.** Mill is referring to the empirical tradition of Locke, Hume and himself, who 'trace up all the elements of happiness, as they do all those of the intellect, to the simple sensations', and to Kant, Reid and Dugald Stewart, who for various reasons admit 'truths . . . which the mind recognizes without the aid of the senses'.

9. p. 68, **Helvétius.** Clause Adrien Helvétius (1715–71), one of the encyclopedists. His work on educational theory—*De l'homme, de ses facultés intellectuelles, et de son éducation*—only appeared after his death in 1772. There is much similarity between his thinking and that of James Mill: both adopted the same definition of education, both were extreme environmentalists, both accepted Locke's empiricism and both were hedonists.

10. p. 69, **Rousseau.** Jean-Jacques Rousseau (1702–78), French political philosopher. His educational theories are set out in *Emile*, 1762.

11. p. 69, **Jones.** Sir William Jones (1746–94), the Sanskrit scholar and a friend of Johnson, Gibbon and Burke.

12. p. 73, **Darwin.** Dr Erasmus Darwin (1731–1802), grandfather of Charles Darwin; spent most of his life as a physician at Lichfield where he established a botanical garden. In his *Zoönomia* (1794–6) he expounds the laws of organic life on the evolutionary principle.

13. p. 73, **Cabanis.** Pierre Cabanis (1757–1808), a follower of Condillac; developed the physiological side of sense-experience.

14. p. 88, **Dr Crichton.** Sir Alexander Crichton (1763–1856), physician to Czar Alexander I of Russia. His book on *Mental Derangement* appeared in 1798.

15. p. 89, **Dr Smith.** Adam Smith (1723–90), Scottish economist and philosopher. His work, *The Wealth of Nations*, 1776, set out the *laissez-faire* theory of economics which was substantially adopted by Ricardo, Mill and other utilitarians.

16. p. 98, **Miss Edgeworth.** Maria Edgeworth (1767–1849), an educationist who, jointly with her father, wrote *Practical Education* (1798). Mill sent her a copy of Bentham's *Chrestomathia*, in the hope of enlisting her support.

17. p. 108, **Chrestomathia.** The word means 'useful learning'. The book contained a complete secondary school curriculum and a detailed justification of the monitorial system, with acknowledgements to Bell's *Elements of Tuition*, rather than to Joseph Lancaster. It was intended as a blue-print for a secondary day school in London—a project warmly supported by Mill, Place and Ricardo, which failed for lack of funds. *Chrestomathia* also contains major contributions to linguistic theory, a field in which Bentham had remarkably little influence on James Mill. Cf. C. K. Ogden, *Bentham's Theory of Fictions*, London, 1932.

18. p. 112, **d'Alembert.** J. B. d'Alembert (1717–83), editor of *L'Encyclopédie* to which Helvétius contributed. It was sternly rational and sceptical in its views and aroused the hostility of the clergy.

19. p. 113, **Wolf.** Christian Wolf of Marburg. The quotation is from his *Philosophia Rationalis sive Logica* (1728).

Schools for All

The Philanthropist, in which *Schools for All* was first published, was a quarterly journal founded in 1811 by William Allen, a Quaker chemist of Plough Lane. Its full title was: *The Philanthropist, or Repository for hints and suggestions calculated to promote the Comfort and Happiness of Man.* James Mill was an active contributor and, with Allen, who provided the finance, was its mainstay for the first seven years. Mill's ability to work harmoniously with people of strong religious conviction should be noted.

20. p. 124, **Dr Marsh.** Dr Herbert Marsh (1757–1839): in 1807 Lady Margaret Professor of Divinity at Cambridge, 1816 Bishop of Llandaff, 1819 Bishop of Peterborough. A High Church opponent of the Evangelical Movement who in 1811 attacked the proposal to establish a Bible Society at Cambridge, on the grounds that the Bible should not be read without its Anglican interpretation. His opposition to Lancaster logically followed, and he was largely responsible for founding the National Society for Church of England Schools in 1811. Marsh was not the first Anglican opponent of Lancaster: in 1805 Mrs Trimmer had denounced non-Anglican schools as sowing the seeds of revolution. Marsh at first was unrepresentative of general Anglican opinion, but later, the National Schools Society commanded widespread support among the bishops.

21. p. 129, **Anti-Jacobin Review.** Mill's first employment as a journalist was with this review, but he was then more conventional and right-wing than he subsequently became.

22. p. 131, **Mr Davy.** Presumably Mr, later Sir Humphrey, Davy (1778–1829), who as professor of chemistry at the Royal Institution attracted large audiences to his lectures. He is familiar to students of economic history as the inventor of the miner's safety-lamp.

23. p. 142, **Dr Paley.** William Paley (1743–1805), a famous utilitarian theologian: it was natural that Mill should find useful support from his writings but he was far from representative of Anglican opinion.

24. p. 142, **Mr Windham.** William Windham of Norfolk, M.P., 1784, member of Pitt's administration, 1794.

25. p. 175, **Test Act.** The Test Acts of 1673 and 1678 made communion with Established Church, and repudiation of Roman Catholic doctrine, a condition of eligibility to all civil or military offices.

26. p. 181, **The Quarterly Review.** Founded 1809 by J. Murray the publisher as a Tory rival to the *Edinburgh Review*. It represented Tory and High Church opinion.

27. p. 191. It is interesting to notice that Mill here advocates common schools to reduce religious divisions in society in the same way as many advocate comprehensive schools today to promote social unity.

BIBLIOGRAPHICAL NOTE

The standard work on the early utilitarians is E. Halévy, *Growth of Philosophical Radicalism* (London, 1928); an older book, still valuable, is Sir Leslie Stephen, *The English Utilitarians* (3 vols., London, 1900), especially vol. II on James Mill. Both books contain extensive discussions of Mill's educational theories. A full and critical account of the origins of utilitarianism is contained in J. Plamenatz, *The English Utilitarians* (Oxford, 1949). Bertrand Russell, *Freedom and Organization, 1814–1914* (London, 1934), contains a stimulating discussion of the philosophical radicals, including a chapter on James Mill. In studying James Mill, it is important to gain some knowledge of the historical context in which he wrote, and for this E. Halévy, *History of the English People*, Vol. I (London, 1924 and 1961) is indispensable. R. J. White, *From Waterloo to Peterloo* (London, 1957), is also valuable. For Mill's educational theory, it is important to read John Stuart Mill's *Autobiography* (World's Classics, Oxford, 1924) which contains a detailed account of his own education, and with it the early chapters of M. St. J. Packe, *Life of J. S. Mill* (London, 1954). Graham Wallas, *Life of Francis Place* (London, 1898) gives an account of the 'Schools for All' movement, and H. H. Bellot, *University College, London* (London, 1929), contains relevant information on Mill's later educational activities.

A. Bain wrote *James Mill: a biography* (London, 1882) which, if somewhat unselective, is very detailed and is an important source, since Bain consulted J. S. Mill and others who knew James Mill. P. Sraffa (ed.), *Works and Correspondence of David Ricardo*, Vols. VI–IX (Cambridge, 1955), contains many valuable letters. The principal unpublished sources for James Mill are in the Place Collection at the British Museum, with further extensive MSS. in the Manuscripts Department, and in the Brougham and Bentham Collections at University College, London. Mill's Commonplace Book (4 vols.) is in the London Library.

INDEX

INDEX